Teach Yourself To Play Harmonica

STEVEN MANUS & RON MANUS

Everything you need to know to start playing now!

- **For diatonic and chromatic harmonicas**
- **Teaches you how to play through an easy-to-understand, step-by-step system**
- **Play licks in the styles of your favorite performers**
- **How to choose the right harmonica**

D1360909

Alfred

Cover photo: Jeff Oshiro
Cover design: Martha Widmann

Project editor: Kevin M. Mitchell
Special thanks: Barbara Vogel

CONTENTS

Getting Started

Foreword

The harmonica (also referred to as a "mouthharp" or simply "harp") has been around for over 170 years. In that time, it has developed from being a child's toy to an important instrument in today's music. It's heard in the music of folk, blues, country, bluegrass, rock and even in concert halls with symphony orchestras.

This book will introduce you to all the various music styles, which are illustrated with easy-to-learn, fun-to-play songs. Each song is notated with a handy number/arrow system that makes music reading practical (though not essential). The step-by-step instructions give you the basic skills to play all the styles, and all concepts are explained in simple, straightforward English and illustrated with charts and photographs.

When you complete this book, you will:

- have a working knowledge of both the diatonic and chromatic harmonicas
- understand the fundamentals of reading music
- be able to play in the styles of Bruce Springsteen, Bob Dylan, Billy Joel, Stevie Wonder and many others.

A Short History of the Harmonica

The harmonica was patented by C. F. L. Buschmann in Berlin in 1821, but its origins date back further. In early 19th-century Europe, three instruments were invented that share the common attribute of "free reeds"—the harmonica, the harmonium (a small reed organ) and the accordion. Prior to that time, no instrument used in European music had the free reed.

A *free reed* is a thin tongue of metal that is fastened over an opening through which air is forced either by a bellow (harmonium and accordion) or by the player's lungs (harmonica). The length and thickness of the metal tongue or reed determines its pitch (how low or high it sounds). On a well-made instrument, the pitch of each reed is adjusted by filing it near the tip to raise the pitch or near the base to lower it. The reed will only vibrate if the air stream flows from the fixed end toward the free end. In the harmonica, there are two sets of reeds: half of them fixed to play in one direction; half in the other. This allows for a different set of tones when blowing into the instrument than when drawing the air through it.

Some music historians believe that the free reed concept was first introduced to Europe by a French missionary named Père Amiot. He had traveled to the Far East where he became interested in two similar instruments: the Chinese *sheng* and the Japanese *sho.* The sheng and the sho were mouth organs that used free metal reeds. Vibrations of the reeds were magnified by resonating with acoustically coupled wooden tubes. When samples of these Oriental instruments reached Paris in 1777, they created a great deal of excitement in the music world and led to the development of other free reed instruments, including the harmonica.

Great credit for the popularity of the harmonica must be given to the Hohner Company which was founded at Trossingen, Germany in 1857. Hohner's Marine Band model is still one of the best-selling harmonicas in the world.

European immigrants, particularly Germans, brought the instrument to America in the mid-1800s. The inexpensive, portable harmonica could be played expressively with little or no formal training and gained instant popularity with all people, including America's slave population. Talented musicians soon began experimenting with the instrument's possibilities, learning to create sound effects such as train and animal sounds. The blues expanded the scope of the instrument far beyond what its inventor could have imagined. In the 1940s and '50s, the *Harmonicats* (a group comprised of great harmonica players) gained fame with their unique arrangements of classical pieces, novelty and Tin Pan Alley songs, taking the instrument to new heights.

Today, the harmonica is at the height of its popularity. Its appeal runs from the complex and beautiful classical melodies of Larry Adler to the gutsy blues stylings of Sonny Terry and Sonny Boy Williamson. Country music boasts the wonderful Charlie McCoy; jazz has Toots Thielmann. Stevie Wonder, Bob Dylan and Magic Dick of the J. Geils Band are just a few of the great rockers who play harmonica.

Luckily for the aspiring player, there is a wealth of material available on tapes and CDs for your listening pleasure and inspiration as you teach yourself this fun and versatile instrument.

Types of Harmonicas

The two types of harmonicas are the *diatonic* (dye-a-TON-ic) and the *chromatic* (kro-MAT-ic). The diatonic harmonica (or blues harp) is about 4 inches long with 10 holes. It's amazing how much music can be produced by this small, inexpensive instrument.

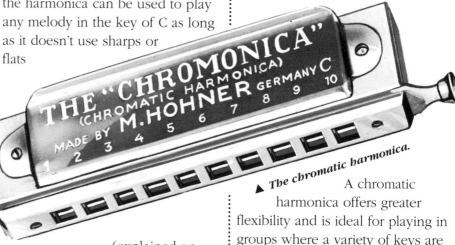

▲ The diatonic harmonica.

The word diatonic means that all the notes on the instrument belong to one scale or key. If you have a harmonica in C (the key is engraved onto the top of the cover on the right), the notes you can play all belong to the C major scale or the key of C. On the piano, this would be the equivalent of only playing on the white keys. Similarly, if you have a harmonica in G, you'll only be able to play notes which belong to the key of G.

You can buy diatonic harmonicas in many keys, which is necessary for a few reasons. If you play with other musicians, they'll be playing in many keys. Guitar players prefer the keys of C, G, D, A, and E; they are easier to play and sound better on that instrument. If you're playing in a band that has trumpets or saxophones, they'll probably prefer keys like F, B♭, E♭ and A♭; these are the most congenial keys for those instruments.

This book uses the C harmonica to demonstrate the instrument.

The 10 holes of the diatonic harmonica can produce 20 notes. Each hole produces one note when you blow and a different note when you draw. Starting with the C below middle C on the piano, the blow notes on the C harmonica are: C E G C E G C E G C. The draw notes are: D G B D F A B D F A.

If you arrange these notes in ascending order, the result (starting with middle C, hole 4) is a two-octave C major scale. In this way, the harmonica can be used to play any melody in the key of C as long as it doesn't use sharps or flats (explained on page 25). Later we'll show you that this limitation can be overcome by advanced techniques. For now, it's enough to know that the diatonic harmonica or harp is the one often heard in rock, folk, blues and country recordings.

The chromatic harmonica is more sophisticated and flexible, but also has some disadvantages. On the plus side, the chromatic harp can be played in any key. Certain effects, such as the trill, are much easier to play on a chromatic. On the minus side, bending notes downward by using the breath is much harder than on a diatonic harmonica. This effect is a must for blues, country and rock playing, so if this is where your main interest is, we recommend a diatonic harmonica.

Choosing a Harmonica

Your first harmonica or harp should be a C harmonica (a diatonic harmonica in the key of C). In addition to being easy to learn, its small size makes it easy to handle for a player with average-sized hands.

▲ The chromatic harmonica.

A chromatic harmonica offers greater flexibility and is ideal for playing in groups where a variety of keys are used. If you have aspirations toward becoming an all-around player, you'll want to master the chromatic. Its greater range and adaptability to play in any key make it a must for jazz and classical music.

They also make a special electronic pickup that attaches directly to the harmonica. These can be plugged directly into an amplifier.

Care and Grooming of the Harmonica

Here are some important tips for the care of your harmonica:

1. Never expose the instrument to extreme heat or cold.

2. Keep the holes clean and clear of any foreign matter such as chewing gum, food particles or pocket fluff. When not playing, keep the harmonica in its pouch or case.

3. Strike the harmonica against your hand, never a hard surface, to get rid of any moisture in the reeds. You should do this after every song.

4. Before playing, warm the harmonica a little with your hands. This will keep the reeds in good condition.

Breaking in Your Harmonica

1. Start playing in the middle of the harmonica: on a diatonic harmonica, holes 4 through 8; on a chromatic, holes 4 through 9.

2. Don't overblow. Start by just breathing into the instrument. Later, when the reeds have loosened up, you'll be able to play louder. Your breath should come from the diaphragm. Practice moving your diaphragm in and out and notice how this fills and empties your lungs. Breathing from your diaphragm will give you more control over your breath and will result in a smoother sound that is less tiring to produce.

3. After you've mastered controlled breathing, you can add the lower and upper notes.

How to Hold the Harmonica

1. Hold the body of the harmonica in your left hand between the thumb and fingers. Make sure the lower numbers are on your left (Fig. 1).

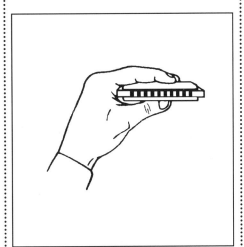

▲ *Fig. 1   Holding the harmonica.*

2. Now fold your right hand over the harmonica, forming a tight cup (Fig. 2).

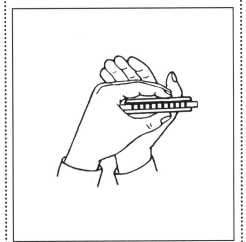

▲ *Fig. 2   Holding the harmonica.*

The chromatic is held the same as the diatonic, except that the right thumb is used to work the slide button.

Vibrato

The Italian word *vibrato* (vye-BRA-toe) means a gentle wavering of the tone. Most instruments and voices use vibrato, as this effect adds warmth and personality to the sound. On the harmonica, vibrato is produced by opening and closing the cupped hands. The speed of the vibrato (opening and closing the hands) is largely a matter of taste, but most players use anywhere between 160 and 240 beats per minute. (If you don't have a metronome, remember that most marching bands play at 120 beats per minute.)

Vibrato can also be produced by moving the whole hand to give a gentle wavering effect (Fig. 3).

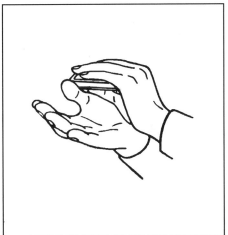

▲ *Fig. 3   Producing vibrato.*

Chording

A *chord* can be defined as three or more notes played together. On the harmonica, you can play a chord by blowing into any three holes. Or, you can draw through any three holes.

Try this on your harp:

Blow into holes 1 2 3	Draw holes 1 2 3
Blow into holes 2 3 4	Draw holes 2 3 4
Blow 3 4 5	Draw 3 4 5
Blow 4 5 6	Draw 4 5 6
Blow 5 6 7	Draw 5 6 7
Blow 6 7 8	Draw 6 7 8
Blow 7 8 9	Draw 7 8 9
Blow 8 9 10	Draw 8 9 10

If you find that you're not accurately covering three holes and getting a good, clear chord, don't worry; you'll gain more control with practice.

Harmonica Notation

There are several different types of harp notation presently in use. We believe the one used in this book is the clearest and easiest to use even if you don't read music.

1. You have already noticed that the holes are numbered at least from 1 to 10. Some models have more holes, and a few have less, but this book will limit itself to 10 on the diatonic. To play a chord, use a group of numbers such as 3 4 5, or 7 8 9, etc. This means to use only those holes.

2. The next important point is the *direction* of the breath.

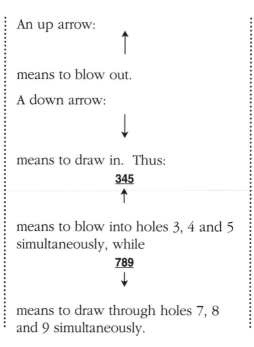

An up arrow:

means to blow out.

A down arrow:

means to draw in. Thus:

345
↑

means to blow into holes 3, 4 and 5 simultaneously, while

789
↓

means to draw through holes 7, 8 and 9 simultaneously.

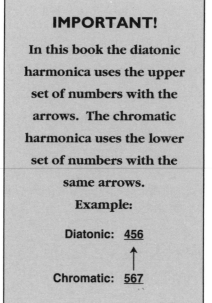

IMPORTANT!

In this book the diatonic harmonica uses the upper set of numbers with the arrows. The chromatic harmonica uses the lower set of numbers with the same arrows.

Example:

Diatonic: **456**
↑
Chromatic: **567**

The *length* of the stem on an arrow suggests how long the note or chord should last.

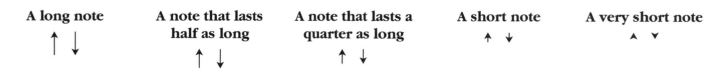

A long note	**A note that lasts half as long**	**A note that lasts a quarter as long**	**A short note**	**A very short note**
↑ ↓	↑ ↓	↑ ↓	↑ ↓	↑ ↓

Here's what "Jingle Bells" looks like in this type of notation.

Jingle Bells Track 1

	Jin -	gle	bells,	jin -	gle	bells,	jin -	gle	all	the	way,
Diatonic:	345	345	345	345	345	345	345	456	234	234	345
	↑	↑	↑	↑	↑	↑	↑	↑	↑	↓	↑
Chromatic:	456	456	456	456	456	456	456	567	345	345	456

	Oh	what	fun	it	is	to	ride	in	a	one -	horse	o -	pen	sleigh,	hey!
Diatonic:	345	345	345	345	345	345	345	345	345	345	234	234	345	234	456
	↓	↓	↓	↓	↓	↑	↑	↑	↑	↑	↓	↓	↑	↓	↑
Chromatic:	456	456	456	456	456	456	456	456	456	456	345	345	456	345	567

	Jin -	gle	bells,	jin -	gle	bells,	jin -	gle	all	the	way,
Diatonic:	345	345	345	345	345	345	345	456	234	234	345
	↑	↑	↑	↑	↑	↑	↑	↑	↑	↓	↑
Chromatic:	456	456	456	456	456	456	456	567	345	345	456

	Oh	what	fun	it	is	to	ride	on	a	one -	horse	o -	pen	sleigh!
Diatonic:	345	345	345	345	345	345	345	345	345	456	456	345	234	234
	↓	↓	↓	↓	↓	↑	↑	↑	↑	↑	↑	↓	↓	↑
Chromatic:	456	456	456	456	456	456	456	456	456	567	567	456	345	345

Chording Exercises and Songs

The following exercises and songs will help you become familiar with the arrow/number system of notation. This system is used throughout this book to teach material. It will also come in handy in jotting down your ideas as you play and practice.

Row, Row, Row Your Boat Track 2

	Row,	row,	row	your	boat	gent -	ly	down	the	stream;
Diatonic:	234	234	234	234	345	345	234	345	345	456
	↑	↑	↑	∨	↑	↑	∨	↓	∨	↑
Chromatic:	345	345	345	345	456	456	345	456	456	567

Mer -	ri -	ly,	mer -	ri -	ly,	mer -	ri -	ly,	mer -	ri -	ly,	life	is	but	a	dream.
567	567	567	456	456	456	345	345	345	234	234	234	456	345	345	234	234
↑	↑	↑	↑	↑	↑	↑	↑	↑	↑	↑	↑	∨	↑	∨	↑
678	678	678	567	567	567	456	456	456	345	345	345	567	456	456	345	345

Oh! Susanna Track 3

	Oh	I	come	from	Al	a -	bam -	a	with	a	ban -	jo	on	my	knee
Diatonic:	234	234	345	456	456	456	456	345	234	234	345	345	234	234	234
	▲	▼	↑	↑	↑	↓	↑	↑	↑	↓	↑	↑	↓	↑	↓
Chromatic:	345	345	456	567	567	567	567	456	345	345	456	456	345	345	345

	I'm——		goin'	to	Lou -	si -	an -	a	my		true	love	for	to	see
	234	234	345	456	456	456	456	345	234	234	345	345	234	234	234
	▲	▼	↑	↑	↑	↓	↑	↑	▲	▼	↑	↑	↓	↓	↑
	234	234	345	456	456	456	456	345	234	234	456	456	345	345	345

	It——		rained	all	night	the	day	I	left	the	wea -	ther	it	was	dry
	234	234	345	456	456	456	456	456	456	456	345	345	234	234	234
	▲	▼	↑	↑	↑	↓	↑	↑	↑	↓	↑	↑	↓	↑	↓
	345	345	456	567	567	567	567	456	345	345	456	456	345	345	345

	the——		sun	so	hot	I	froze	to	death,	Su -	san -	na	don't	you	cry.
	234	234	345	456	456	456	456	345	234	234	345	345	234	234	234
	▲	▼	↑	↑	↑	↓	↑	↑	↑	↓	↑	↑	↓	↓	↑
	345	345	456	567	567	567	567	456	345	345	456	456	345	345	345

	Oh!	Su -	san -	na,	Oh!	don't	you	cry	for	me
	345	345	456	456	456	456	456	345	234	234
	↓	↓	↓	↓	↓	↓	↑	↑	↑	↓
	345	345	456	456	567	567	567	456	345	345

	'Cause	I	come	from	Al	a -	bam -	a	with	my	ban -	jo	on	my	knee.
	234	234	345	456	456	456	456	345	234	234	345	345	234	234	234
	▲	▼	↑	↑	↑	↓	↑	↑	↑	↓	↑	↑	↓	↓	↑
	345	345	456	567	567	567	567	456	345	345	456	456	345	345	345

Playing Single Notes

Although single notes are harder to play than chords, they must be mastered in order to play melodies and blues-rock leads.

There are two ways to play single notes on the harmonica. Pick the one you find easier and stick with it! Some practice now will serve you well later.

Tonguing

This is the best way to play if you'll be playing a chromatic harp.

1. Blow into holes 4, 5 and 6, making a chord.

2. Push your tongue forward against the holes so that only one hole is uncovered and sounds. This can be either to the left or right of your tongue (hole 4 or 6), *but pick a side and stick to it.*

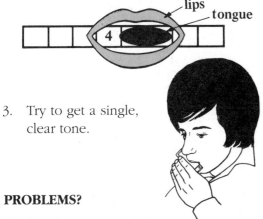

3. Try to get a single, clear tone.

PROBLEMS?

Getting the wrong note?
  Try placing the tip of your tongue in the hole (hole 5) next to the one you want to play. Press the side of your tongue against the other unplayed hole.

Getting two notes?
  You're not covering both holes.

1. Problem →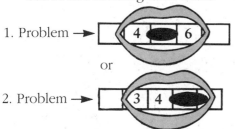

  or

2. Problem →

Try moving the harmonica very slightly to the left or right, making sure that you're still blowing into hole 4.

Puckering

Many who pick up on the harmonica play this way.

1. Tighten your lips as if to whistle and blow into hole 4. Do not use your tongue.

2. Try getting a single, clear tone.

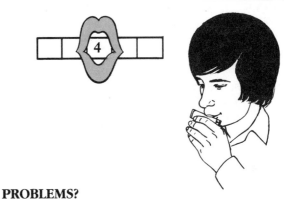

PROBLEMS?

Can't get one note?

1. Problem →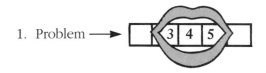

Tighten your lips and press them more firmly against the harp.

2. Problem →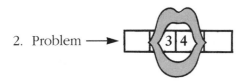

A common problem with this method is getting the pucker over the hole. Try moving the harmonica slightly to the right or left in order to better center your mouth over the hole.

Here are some exercises to practice. They will help you produce single notes clearly. Remember: diatonic uses the upper numbers/arrows; chromatic uses the lower numbers/arrows.

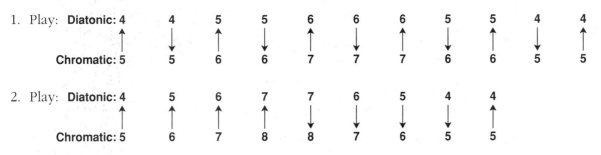

1. Play: **Diatonic:** 4 ↑ 4 ↓ 5 ↑ 5 ↓ 6 ↑ 6 ↓ 6 ↑ 5 ↓ 5 ↑ 4 ↓ 4 ↑
          Chromatic: 5 5 6 6 7 7 7 6 6 5 5

2. Play: **Diatonic:** 4 ↑ 5 ↑ 6 ↑ 7 ↑ 7 ↓ 6 ↓ 5 ↓ 4 ↓ 4 ↑
          Chromatic: 5 6 7 8 8 7 6 5 5

Single-Note Exercises

Practicing these exercises will prepare you for the single-note material that follows. These tips will help you get the maximum benefit from the exercises:

1. If you have access to a metronome, set it to a medium beat (between 80 and 120 beats per minute). Play the exercises with one beat for each medium-sized arrow ↑ ; two beats for the longer arrows ↑ ; and four beats for the longest arrows ↑ . If you find it impossible to use a metronome, tap your foot to a moderate walking beat and use that. *It is important to keep a steady beat!*

2. Make sure you're playing one note at a time. If you're having trouble doing this, refer to the "Problems?" section on the previous page.

3. Don't overblow the harp. Breathing nice and easy from the diaphragm will get the best sound.

Only two different length arrows are used on this page: ↑ = 1 beat; ↑ = 2 beats.

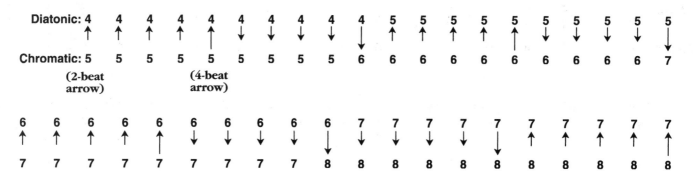

What you have just played is called a C major scale.

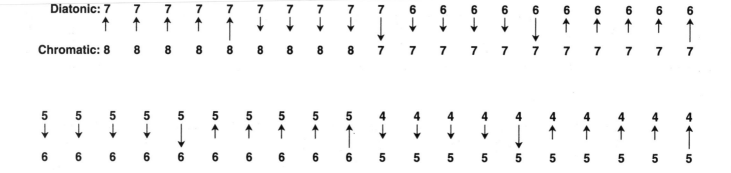

What you have just played is the C major scale, descending.

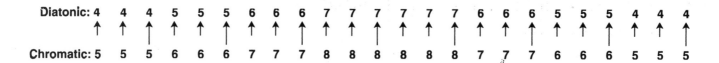

This exercise jumps from hole to hole. This makes it a little more difficult than the previous ones, but the technique you develop will be useful in playing real songs.

Diatonic: 4	4	6	6	8	8	7	9	9	7	7	8	6	7
↑	↑	↑	↑	↑	↑	↑	↓	↓	↓	↓	↑	↑	↑
Chromatic: 5	5	7	7	10	10	8	10	10	8	8	10	7	8

On this page and page 12, you'll find music that makes use of the single-note technique. You're probably familiar with most of the melodies. (This will make it easier for you to get the correct timing for the notes.)

Ode to Joy Track 4

Joyously

Diatonic: 5	5	5	6	6	5	5	4	4	4	4	5	5	4	4	5	5	5	6	6	5	5	4	4	4	4	5	4	4	4
↑	↑	↓	↑	↓	↑	↓	↑	↓	↑	↓	↑	↓	↑	↓	↑	↑	↓	↑	↓	↑	↓	↑	↓	↑	↓	↑	↓	↑	↑
Chromatic: 6	6	6	7	7	6	6	5	5	5	5	6	6	5	5	6	6	6	7	7	6	6	5	5	5	5	6	5	5	5

Down in the Valley Track 5

Plaintively (Use plenty of vibrato on the long notes—see page 5 for how to produce the vibrato.)

Down	in	the	val -	ley,	val -	ley	so	low,	hang	your	head	o -	ver,	hear	the	wind	blow.
Diatonic: 3	4	4	5	4	5	4	4	4	3	3	4	5	4	3	4	4	4
↑	↑	↓	↑	↑	↑	↓	↑	↓	↑	↓	↓	↓	↓	↓	↑	↓	↑
Chromatic: 3	5	5	6	5	6	5	5	5	3	4	5	6	5	4	5	5	5

Hear	the	wind	blow,	boys,	hear	the	wind	blow,	Hang	your	head	o -	ver,	hear	the	wind	blow.
3	4	4	5	4	5	4	4	4	3	3	4	5	4	3	4	4	4
↑	↑	↓	↑	↑	↑	↓	↑	↓	↑	↓	↓	↓	↓	↓	↑	↓	↑
3	5	5	6	5	6	5	5	5	3	4	5	6	5	4	5	5	5

When the Saints Go Marching In Track 6

With spirit

Oh	when	the	saints	go	march -	ing	in,	Oh	when	the	saints	go	march -	ing	in,
Diatonic: 4	5	5	6	4	5	5	6	4	5	5	6	5	4	5	4
↑	↑	↓	↑	↑	↑	↓	↑	↑	↑	↓	↑	↑	↑	↑	↓
Chromatic: 5	6	6	7	5	6	6	7	5	6	6	7	6	5	6	5

Oh,	Lord,	I	want	to	be	in	that	num -	ber,	when	the	saints	go	march - ing	in.
5	5	4	4	4	5	6	6	6	5	5	5	6	5	4	4	4
↑	↑	↓	↑	↑	↑	↑	↑	↑	↓	↑	↓	↑	↑	↑	↓	↑
6	6	5	5	5	6	7	7	7	6	6	6	7	6	5	5	5

He's Got the Whole World in His Hands Track 7

Moderate gospel tempo

He's	got	the	whole	world___		in	His	hands,	He's	got	the	whole	world___		in	His	hands,
Diatonic: 6	6	6	6	5	4	6	6	6	6	6	6	5	4	3	6	6	6
↑	↑	↑	↑	↑	↑	↑	↓	↑	↑	↑	↓	↓	↓	↑	↓	↑
Chromatic: 7	7	7	7	6	5	7	7	7	7	7	6	5	4	7	7	7

He's	got	the	whole	world___		in	His	hands,	He's	got	the	whole	world	in	His	hands.
6	6	6	6	5	4	6	6	6	6	6	6	6	6	5	4	4
↑	↑	↑	↑	↑	↑	↑	↓	↑	↑	↑	↑	↑	↑	↓	↓	↑
7	7	7	7	6	5	7	7	7	7	7	7	7	7	6	5	5

Silent Night Track 8

Gently (use vibrato throughout)

	Si	- lent	night,	ho	- ly	night,	All	is	calm,	all	is	bright.
Diatonic:	6↑	6↓	6↑	5↓	6↑	6↓	6↑	5↓	8↓	8↓	7↓	7↑	7↑	6↑
Chromatic:	7	7	7	6	7	7	7	6	9	9	8	8	8	7

	'Round	yon	Vir	- gin	Moth	- er	and	child,	Ho	- ly	in	- fant	so	ten	- der	and	mild,
	6↓	6↓	7↑	7↓	6↓	6↑	6↓	6↑	5↑	6↓	6↓	7↑	7↓	6↓	6↑	6↓	6↑	5↑
	7	7	8	8	7	7	7	7	6	7	7	8	8	7	7	7	7	6

	Sleep	in	heav	- en	- ly	peace___	sleep___	in	heav	- en	- ly	peace.
	8↓	8↓	9↓	8↓	7↓	7↑	8↑	7↑	6↑	5↑	6↑	5↓	4↓	4↑
	9	9	10	9	8	9	10	8	7	6	7	6	5	5

Clementine Track 9

Moderately, with spirit

	In	a	cav	- ern,	in	a	can	- yon	ex	- ca	- vat	- ing	for	a	mine,
Diatonic:	4↑	4▲	4↑	3↑	5↑	5▲	5↑	4↑	4↑	5▲	6↑	6↑	5↓	5▲	4↓
Chromatic:	4	4	4	3	6	6	6	5	5	6	7	7	6	6	5

	Lived	a	min	- er	for	- ty	nin	- er,	and	his	daugh	- ter,	Clem	- en	- tine.
	4↓	5▲	5↓	5↓	5↑	4▼	5↑	4↑	4↑	5▲	4↓	3↑	3↓	4▼	4↑
	5	6	6	6	6	5	6	5	5	6	5	3	4	5	5

	Oh,	my	dar	- lin',	oh,	my	dar	- lin',	oh,	my	dar	- lin'	Clem	- en	- tine,
	4↑	4▲	4↑	3↑	5↑	5▲	5↑	4↑	4↑	5▲	6↑	6↑	5↓	5▲	4↓
	4	4	4	3	6	6	6	5	5	6	7	7	6	6	5

	You	are	lost	and	gone	for	- ev	- er,	dread	- ful	sor	- ry	Clem	- en	- tine.
	4↓	5▲	5↓	5↓	5↑	4▼	5↑	4↑	4↑	5▲	4↓	3↑	3↓	4▼	4↑
	5	6	6	6	6	5	6	5	5	6	5	3	4	5	5

GETTING ACQUAINTED WITH MUSIC NOTATION

Standard music notation is often used for the harmonica. Although it may take a little getting used to, standard notation is more precise and flexible than the number/arrow system we have been using. Music books and sheet music use standard notation, so it should be known and understood by aspiring, well-rounded harmonica players. Yet the number/arrow system is valuable in showing you the breathing and position of every note.

In this book, we'll give you the best of both worlds: from this page on, every song will be written out in standard notation and the number/arrow system.

Notes

The shape of the note tells you how long to play it. The open note is held the longest; the open notes with stems are played twice as fast; and the closed notes with stems, four times as fast as the open note, and so on. The closed notes with double beams are the fastest-played notes in this book.

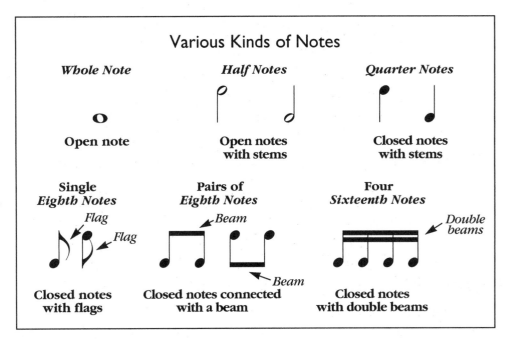

How high or low a note is played is determined by its position on a five-line staff. Notes can be placed on a line or in a space between the lines. The notes are named A B C D E F G. No other letters are used.

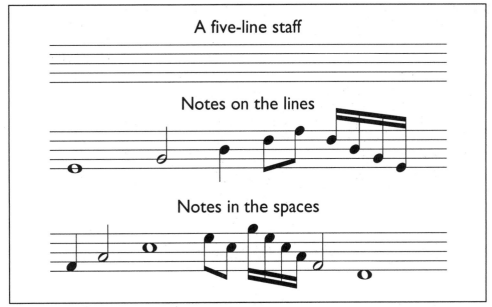

Rests

Rests are measured silences used in music. Here are the most commonly used rests. The longest rest, the whole rest, is to the left, and indicates four beats of silence. The length of each rest gets shorter as you move to the right.

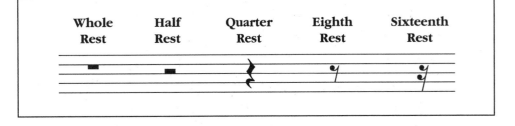

CLEFS

In order to identify the notes on the five-line staff, a symbol called a *clef* is placed at the beginning of each staff.

Most music for the harmonica is written on the treble clef, also called the G clef. It looks like this:

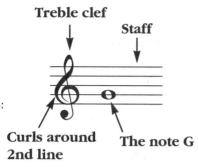

Treble clef

Staff

Curls around 2nd line

The note G

The bass (pronounced: base) clef is used for the lowest notes on the harmonica. The bass clef, also called the F clef, looks like this:

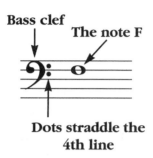

Bass clef

The note F

Dots straddle the 4th line

Naming the Notes in the Treble Clef

Notes that are higher on the staff sound higher.

NOTES ON THE LINES:

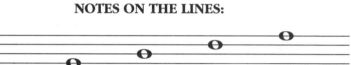

E   G   B   D   F

NOTES IN THE SPACES:

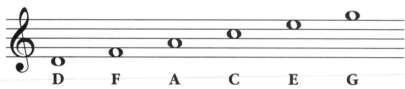

D   F   A   C   E   G

The following memory tricks may help you remember the notes:
On the lines (from bottom to top): Every Good Boy Does Fine
In the spaces (from bottom to top): Don't Forget All Cows Eat Grass

Naming the Notes in the Bass Clef

NOTES ON THE LINES:

G   B   D   F   A

NOTES IN THE SPACES:

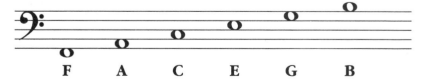

F   A   C   E   G   B

Memory tricks for the bass clef:
On the lines: Good Boys Do Fine Always
In the spaces: F A C E Good Bye

BASIC RHYTHM

As we have seen, the pitch of a note (how high or low it is) is indicated by its position on the five-line staff. The duration of a note (how long it sounds) is indicated by its shape. Imagine a steady beat, like a clock ticking. Tap your foot to this beat. In the following exercises, play any note. The stem direction (up and down) is determined by its position on the staff.

Quarter notes are closed notes with stems. Blow into your harmonica once for each tap.

Half notes are played twice as long as quarter notes. Play these half notes on your harmonica and make them last for two taps:

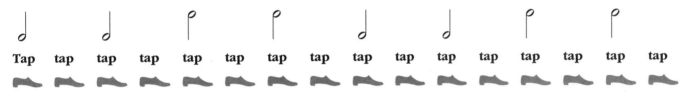

Whole notes are held for four taps:

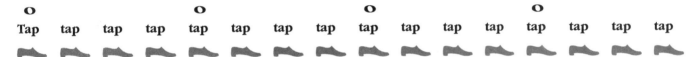

Finally, play some *eighth notes*. They're played twice for every tap. Play the first note as your foot taps down (down beat); play the second note as your foot rises (up beat).

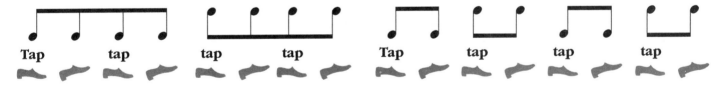

SUMMING UP

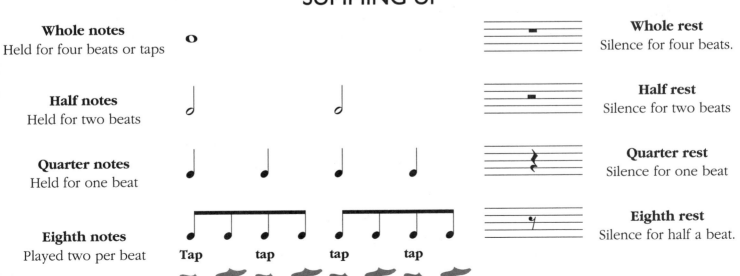

Whole notes
Held for four beats or taps

Half notes
Held for two beats

Quarter notes
Held for one beat

Eighth notes
Played two per beat

Whole rest
Silence for four beats.

Half rest
Silence for two beats

Quarter rest
Silence for one beat

Eighth rest
Silence for half a beat.

MEASURES AND BAR LINES

Bar lines are vertical lines that divide the staff into *measures*. This shows the basic pulse of the music and makes reading music easier by dividing the notes into short groups.

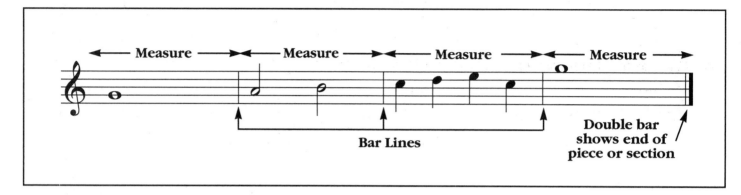

TIME SIGNATURES

At the beginning of every piece of music, immediately after the clef, there's a fraction such as 2/4, 3/4 or 4/4, called a *time signature*.

The upper number indicates how many beats in each measure. In the above example, the time signature is 3/4, so we know there will be three beats in each measure.

The lower number indicates what type of note gets one beat. In the above example, the lower number is a 4, so we know that each quarter note will get one beat.

Here are some examples of rhythms you'll find in various time signatures. Play them on your harmonica.

In 2/4 time, there are always two quarter-note beats in each measure.

In 3/4 time, there are always three quarter notes in each measure. The dot after the half note increases its value by one half, so a *dotted half note* gets a total of three beats.

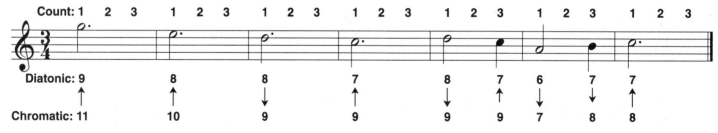

In 4/4 time, there are always four quarter-note beats in a measure.

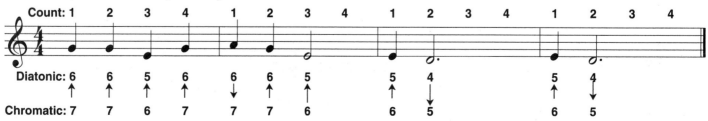

RIDDLES AND QUIZZES

To solve the riddles below, fill in the names of the notes on the lines below them:

1. What did Mary buy to go with her sequined dress?

2. What was the sheriff wearing after ten years in the desert?

3. What did Johnny take to get to Carnegie Hall?

4. But he didn't enjoy the concert.
A head cold made him:

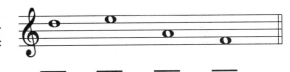

5. A description of Darth Vader.

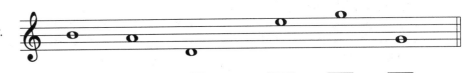

6. Sally shouldn't have told Gabriel her secret. Why?

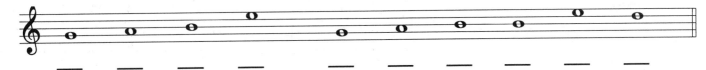

In the examples below, some beats have been omitted. Fill them in with notes and/or rests and complete the measures. (There are several correct answers.)

For answers, see page 71.

PART II   Jukebox

On pages 18–27, you'll find a collection of songs in different styles. Each song is arranged in traditional notation as well as the arrow/number system. Play through and practice each song, as all are designed to enhance your playing by stressing a particularly important musical technique.

Careless Love
Use vibrato on this blues-influenced song.

Take Me Out to the Ball Game Track 12

This song introduces the *tie*. When two notes of the same pitch are connected by a curved line, they are tied. The second note is not played; its value is added to the first note. For example, in measures 7 and 8, the two tied G's are held for a total of five beats (dotted half = 3 beats; a half note = 2 beats; both = 5 beats).

We have simplified the melody so it can be played on a diatonic harmonica.

Norworth and von Tilzer

Home on the Range Track 13

Sometimes a song begins with an incomplete measure called a *pickup*. The pickup measure contains fewer beats than are called for in the time signature. For example, a 4/4 pickup measure may contain one, two or three beats. A 3/4 measure may contain one or two beats and so on. Often (but not always) the last measure of the piece will be missing the same number of beats that the pickup uses. In this way the initial incomplete measure is completed.

Look at the last measure of *Home on the Range*. It has only two beats. These two beats, plus the one beat in the pickup measure (the first measure), complete one measure of 3/4 time. A pickup measure is introduced in this famous cowboy song.

Higley and Kelley

Here are two more songs that use the dotted quarter note. If you're having trouble with this rhythm, try marking the dot by tapping your foot:

Count: 1 & 2 & 3 & 4 & | 1 & 2 & 3   4

This will help you coordinate the rhythm with the beat.

Michael, Row the Boat Ashore

Traditional

Over There  Track 16

This famous World War I song begins with a two-beat pickup in 4/4 time. Notice that the last measure only has two beats, completing one measure.

George M. Cohan

Bright march tempo

* Chromatic sounds an octave lower than written.

Are You from Dixie?

This country classic was a big hit for Chet Atkins and Jerry Reed.

Yellen and Cobb

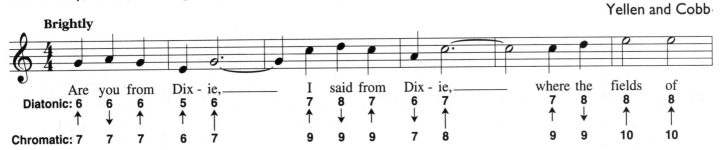

Brightly

	Are	you	from	Dix -	ie,	I	said	from	Dix -	ie,	where the	fields	of
Diatonic:	6	6	6	5	6	7	8	7	6	7	7	8	8	8
Chromatic:	7	7	7	6	7	9	9	9	7	8	9	9	10	10

cot -	ton	beck -	on	to	me?	I'm	glad	to	see	you,	tell	me	how
8	8	8	8	7	6	6	6	6	5	6	7	8	7
10	10	10	9	8	7	7	7	7	6	7	9	9	9

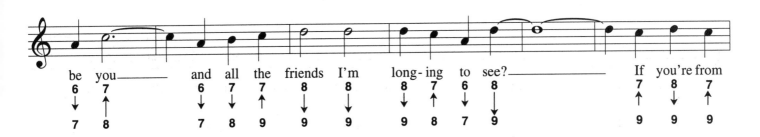

be	you	and	all	the	friends	I'm	long-ing	to	see?	If	you're from
6	7	6	7	7	8	8	8	7	6	8	7	8	7
7	8	7	8	9	9	9	9	8	7	9	9	9	9

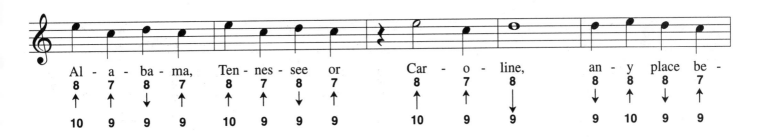

Al -	a -	ba -	ma,	Ten -	nes -	see	or	Car -	o -	line,	an -	y	place	be -
8	7	8	7	8	7	8	7	8	7	8	8	8	8	7
10	9	9	9	10	9	9	9	10	9	9	9	10	9	9

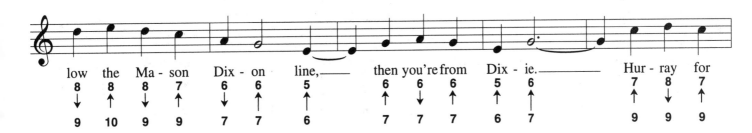

low	the	Ma -	son	Dix -	on	line,	then	you're from	Dix -	ie.	Hur -	ray	for
8	8	8	7	6	6	5	6	6	6	5	6	7	8	7
9	10	9	9	7	7	6	7	7	7	6	7	9	9	9

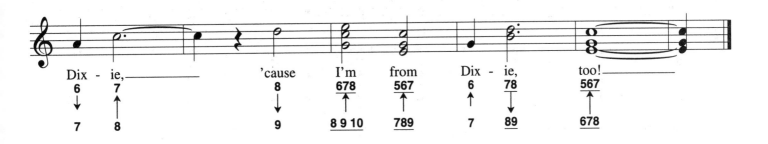

Dix -	ie,	'cause	I'm	from	Dix -	ie,	too!
6	7	8	**678**	**567**	6	**78**	**567**
7	8	9	**8 9 10**	**789**	7	**89**	**678**

Worried Man Blues  Track 18
(It Takes a Worried Man to Sing a Worried Song)

Junior Wells

SHARPS, FLATS AND NATURALS

A **sharp** (♯) is a symbol used to show that a note has been *raised* one half step. The note between F and G is F♯ (say: F-sharp). A **flat** (♭) is a symbol used to show that a note has been *lowered* one half step. The note between A and B is B♭ (say: B-flat). A **natural** (♮) is a symbol that indicates that a note is neither sharp nor flat and is often used to "cancel out" the sign that's in the key signature (for that note only).

The **key** of a song is determined by its *key signature*. The key signature is one or more sharps or flats placed immediately after each clef (when there are no sharps or flats, it means the song is in the key of C). In the next song the key signature consists of one sharp placed on the F line of the staff. This means that every F in the piece is played as F♯. (Since this particular song doesn't have an F in it, you don't need to do anything differently than you have been doing.)

Ordinarily a piece with an F# in the key signature is said to be in the key of G major. (For further information about other keys, see page 38.)

Cross Harp

Cross Harp means playing the harmonica in a different key than that of the instrument. Playing a song in the key of G on a C harmonica is an example of cross harp.

Red River Valley

Vibrato is appropriate for this famous cowboy song. By the way, the Red River the song refers to is the one in Canada, not the better known river in Texas.

Traditional

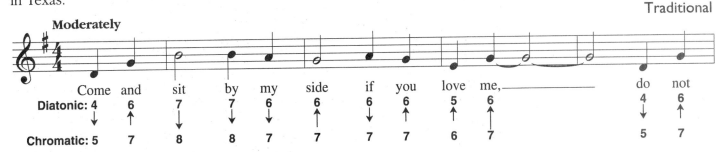

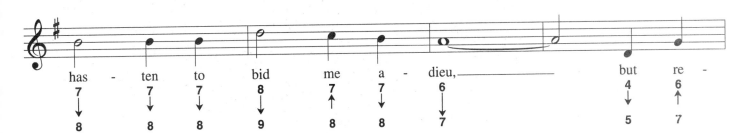

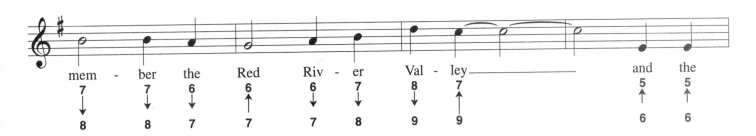

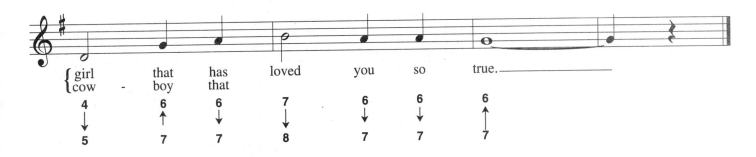

Tom Dooley *Track 20*

(Words and music collected, adapted and arranged by Frank Warner, John A. Lomax and Alan Lomax. From the singing of Frank Proffitt.)

The Kingston Trio recording of this song was the biggest hit of the folk revival of the '50s and '60s.

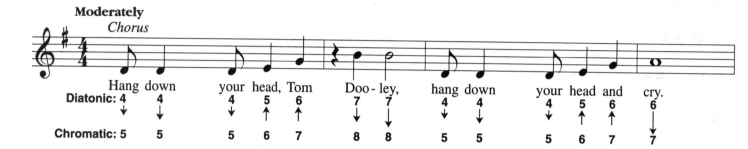

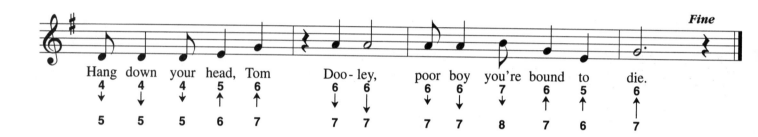

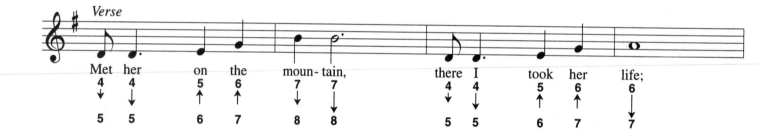

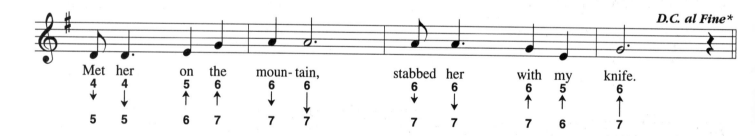

Additional Verses

2. This time tomorrow, reckon where I'll be?
   Hadn' a been for Grayson,
   I'd-a been in Tennessee.
   (Repeat Chorus)

3. This time tomorrow, reckon where I'll be?
   Down in some lonesome valley,
   hangin' from a white oak tree.
   (Repeat chorus to the word "Fine")

*D.C. al Fine stands for *Da Capo al Fine* (Dah CAH-po al Fee-nay), which is a musical term of Italian origin. It means to go back to the beginning of the piece and play through to the word *Fine*. At the end of this particular piece, return to the beginning, then stop at the end of the second line.

Good Night, Irene

Track 21

Huddie Ledbetter, known as blues legend Leadbelly, started playing this song around 1917. The Weavers, a famous folk group of the '40s and '50s, had a big hit with it in 1950.

Words and Music by
Huddie Ledbetter and
John Lomax

Additional Verses

2. Sometimes I live in the country,
Sometimes I live in the town.
Sometimes I have a great notion
To jump into the river and drown.
(Repeat Chorus)

3. Stop ramblin', stop your gamblin',
Stop stayin' out late at night.
Go home to your wife and your fam'ly,
Sit down by the fireside bright.
(Repeat Chorus)

PART III

Advanced Techniques

A Brief History of the Blues

The blues grew from the roots of slavery in America and has been evolving ever since. It was first heard around the turn of the century, particularly in the south. Here, musicians like W. C. Handy, Robert Johnson, Blind Lemon Jefferson and others contributed greatly to this uniquely original American music. With the publication of Handy's *St. Louis Blues* in 1914, the blues became an international sensation. Blues recordings sold in the hundreds of thousands, and many musicians took up the expressive music.

Bands that used mostly homemade instruments (called "jug bands") prominently featured the harmonica, and became popular in the 1920s. In the late '20s, pianist and blues singer Leroy Carr brought a new sophistication to the music and influenced blues stars of the '30s and '40s including Big Bill Broonzy and Sonny Boy Williamson. After World War II, Brownie McGhee, Junior Wells, Little Walter, Lightnin' Hopkins, T-Bone Walker, Muddy Waters and great blues harpist Sonny Terry, among others, came into prominence.

In the 1950s, the blues gave birth to rock 'n' roll, and many of rock's early hits were based on the blues. Elvis Presley's *That's All Right, Mama*, Chuck Berry's *Mabellene*, Gene Vincent's *Be Bop a Lula*, Bill Haley's *Rock Around the Clock* and hundreds of others all relied on a 12-bar blues progression.

The harmonica has been an important part of blues and rock since the very beginning, both as a solo voice and as a supporting rhythm instrument. The blues harmonica tradition continues today in the music of Paul Butterfield, Bob Dylan, the J. Geils Band and Stevie Wonder. Seek out these recordings (along with other, older blues players— James Cotton, John Mayall and the others already mentioned) and spend time listening to these great artists.

Blues harp player Sonny Terry in performance with Brownie McGhee.

Photo courtesy of the Institute of Jazz Studies.

The 12-Bar Blues Progression

Chords have a bass note, the root, on which the chord is named. For example, a C *major chord* contains the notes C-E-G. A G major chord contains the notes G-B-D etc.

Another type of chord is called a *7th chord*. These have four notes, but on harmonica usually three or two notes are played. The notes in a G7 chord (say: G seventh, not G seven) are G-B-D-F. On the diatonic harmonica, these are all draw notes (holes 2, 3, 4 and 5). They can be played in any combination for a G7 chord. The D7 contains the notes D-F♯-A-C. Since F♯ is not possible, and D and A are draw notes, this chord is always played as single notes, either a D, an A or a C.

Chords played in a sequence are called a *progression*. The blues progression is often found in a 12-bar (or measure) format in 4/4 time.

The Blues Progression in G

Each chord name represents one measure of 4/4 time.

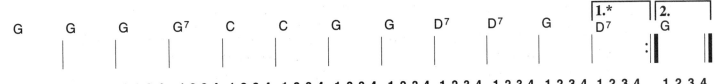

Use the measure under 1 if you want to repeat. Use the measure under 2 for the final ending. This 12-bar progression is the basis for most blues and blues-derived songs in the key of G. Once you know it well, you're on your way to being a great blues harpist!

The following sequence is a 12-bar blues progression in G. Although there is no melody, this can serve as a background for other players' solos. Be sure to count carefully, four beats to each measure. Chord symbols are included for guitar or keyboard accompaniment.

Since virtually all blues is played on diatonic harp, only those numbers are given. Make sure you can play this progression perfectly, without missing a beat before continuing. (Notice that there is a natural sign in this piece. See page 25.)

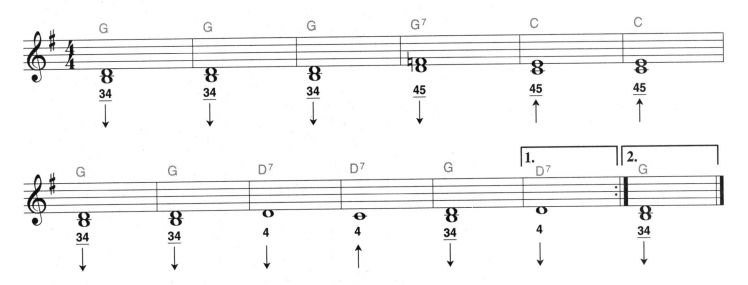

*Play 1st ending the first time only; skip this measure and play 2nd ending on repeat. (See page 62.)

BENDING NOTES

To become a real blues harpist, you've got to learn how to bend notes. It's not easy, but work at it, because it's an important part of the harmonica's vocabulary.

When you bend a note, you are playing it below its true pitch. This technique is heard in blues singing and guitar playing, and you'll hear this effect used often in all kinds of music. Bending notes on the harmonica is a little more difficult—you'll run out of breath quickly—but be patient, work at it and you'll be able to do it.

For Puckerers

1. Draw in from hole 2 as you would normally.

2. As you're doing that, pull your tongue back into your mouth and against the bottom of your jaw. If you suck in hard enough, you might hear the note bend (down in pitch).

3. Try tightening up your lips and jaw. Remember, bending the air column down through your mouth makes notes drop in pitch. So do what's necessary to get the air down along the lower part of your mouth.

For Tonguers

The basic way for you to bend notes is by partially blocking the note with your tongue and bending the air around it. However, it's almost impossible to move your tongue the little amount that's necessary on a small diatonic harp. By drawing in real hard, tightening up the mouth a little and moving the harmonica a little to the right, keeping the tongue to the right of the note being played, you can get the bend.

For Chromatic Harp

Since you can get blues notes by using the slide, all the blues arrangements can be played this way. But a real bluesy sound needs the bending effect, so it'll sound better to play all the blues arrangements in this book on a diatonic harp.

At first, you might just get a slight change in pitch when you bend a note. With practice, the difference will become very noticeable, though the more you bend a note the more air you'll need.

If you can start getting a bend at hole 2, try holes 1 and 3. You'll find that the more you start bending a note, the easier it becomes to bend, because the reeds loosen up.

Some players recommend soaking the harp in water to loosen up the reeds and help in note bending. The Hohner Company warns against this practice—and soaking or boiling their instrument will void the guarantee!

Note Bending and Cross Harp

As previously mentioned, cross harp means playing a song in a key that's different from the one your harmonica is pitched in. For example, you may have noticed that *Red River Valley* on page 25 was in G, but is to be played on a C harp. There is a good reason for this. Typically, the bent notes in the blues are the root, 3rd, 5th and 7th of the key.

In the key of C, these notes are C, E, G and B. Three of these notes are blow notes; only the B is a draw note. As we have learned, it's virtually impossible to bend blow notes. Only the draw notes can be bent. This is why it's difficult, if not impossible, to play a C blues on a C harmonica.

When playing blues in G on a C harmonica, you can bend the notes G, B, D and F, because they are all draw notes (2, 3, 4 and 5). Let's try this out with the basic blues progression. We'll use a curved arrow ↳ to indicate a bent note.

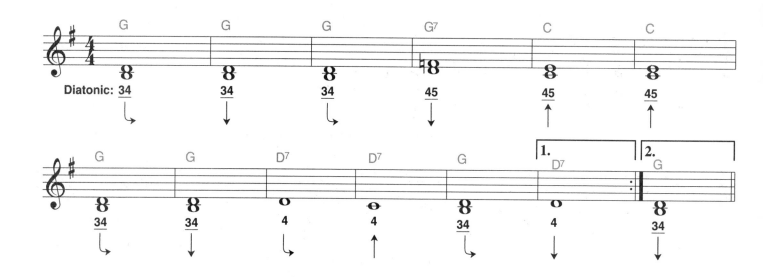

NOTE BENDING (continued)

The following examples continue to use the basic 12-bar blues progression in G, but introduce variations that make it more interesting. Make sure you are counting accurately. Rhythm is important in all music, especially the blues!

Blues background mostly in half notes

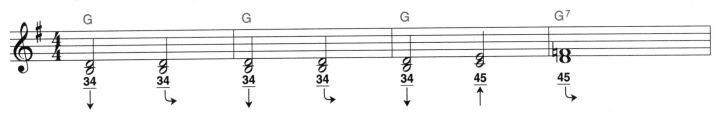

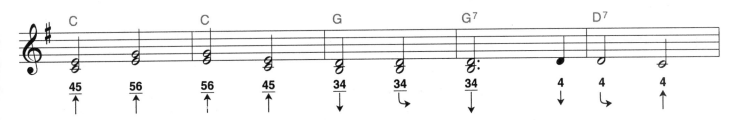

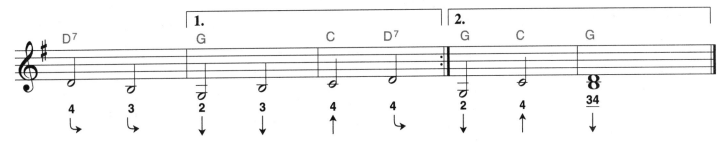

Blues background mostly in quarter notes

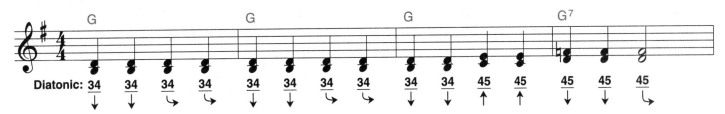

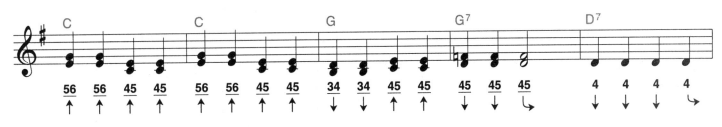

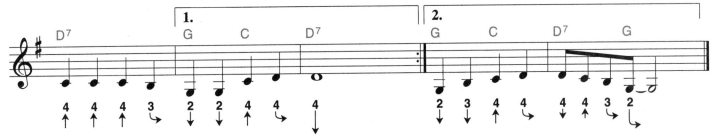

For Chromatic Players: Introducing the Slide Button

While this song is intended as an exercise for teaching diatonic players how to bend notes, you can play the bend by pushing in on the *slide button*. The slide button is used to play all sharps and flats. It is notated by putting a circle around the number:

⑦

Be sure to push the slide button in all the way and then blow or draw. If the chromatic note has a different breath direction than the one for the diatonic note, an additional arrow will appear below it:

⑦
↑

Little Walter

Photo courtesy of the Institute of Jazz Studies.

Blues in G Track 22

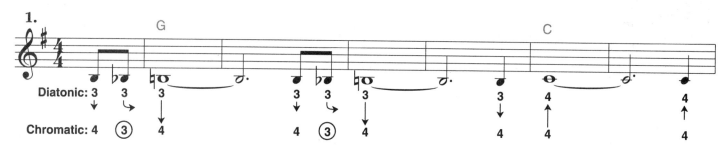

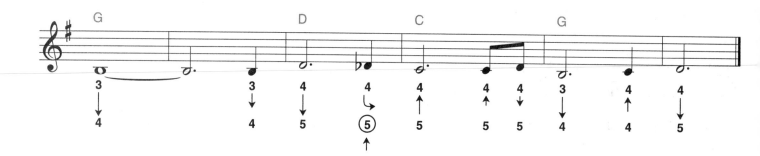

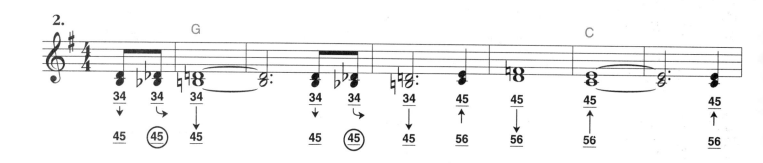

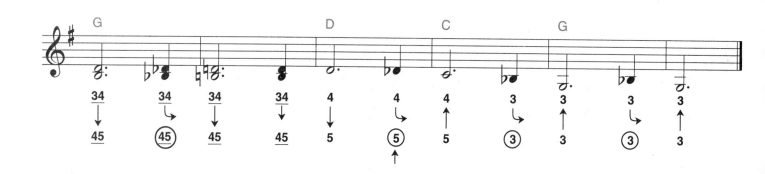

Blues for a Sunday Night Track 23

This original blues tune is based on the 12-bar blues progression with which you've been working. The first chorus has the melody in single notes, with bends used throughout. The second chorus restates the melody, this time in double-note intervals.

Notice a variation in the basic blues progression: in measure 10, C7 replaces D7. This is a common substitution used in many blues tunes.

If you have a friend who plays guitar or keyboard, let him or her play the chords as you play the melody. If you feel adventurous, make up additional choruses of your own.

A typical construction for the blues might be:

1st chorus: Melody in single notes.

2nd chorus: Melody in double notes.

3rd and 4th choruses: Harmonica improvises on chords.

5th and 6th choruses: Guitar player improvises choruses. Harmonica silent.

7th chorus: Repeat 1st chorus and end.

Gambler's Blues

Track 24

Although this blues is in the key of G minor, it can be played cross harp the same as if it was in major.

It was down at Old Joe's Bar room,
At the corner, by the square,
All the drinks were served as usual,
And the usual crowd was there.

On my left stood Joe McKennedy,
His eyes were bloodshot red,
He looked out at the crowd around him,
And these were the words he said:

"Let her go, let her go, God bless her,
Wherever she may be.
She could have searched the wide world
    all over,
And never found a sweet man like me!"

Key to the Highway

Track 25

This great traditional blues* tune can be played cross harp on a C diatonic or a chromatic. When playing blues eighth notes, they are often played unevenly, with a shuffle feel—long-short, long-short, as if you were saying "dunk-a dunk-a" instead of "one and two and."

*Although this blues uses the same chords as the 12-bar blues, it is an 8-bar blues form with the chords in a different order.

Willy the Weeper Track 26

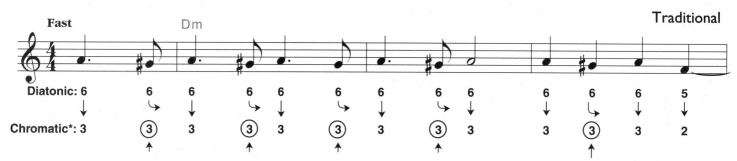

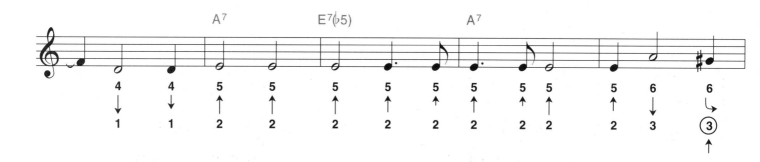

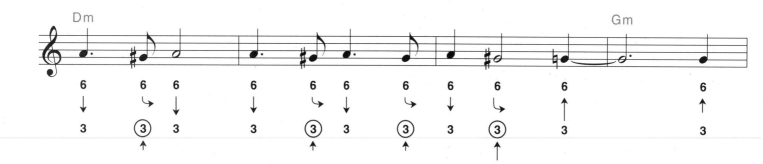

Purely in the interest of sociological research, we present one of many
versions of the lyric to this classic blues tune.

1. Did you ever hear the story 'bout Willy the Weeper?
   He had a job as a chimney sweeper;
   He had the dope habit and he had it bad.
   Now listen while I tell you 'bout the dream he had:

2. At a saloon he swallowed a dozen pills or more
   Then he went 'round the world, from shore to shore.
   The Queen of Sheba was the first one he met;
   Called him tootsie wootsie and her honey pet.

3. He met Cleopatra, she gave him jewels and money
   Dusky beauties in Turkey called him honey;
   In Honolulu he got an automobile
   With a diamond headlight and a golden wheel.

4. He landed in New York one evening late,
   He asked his sugar for an after date;
   He started to kiss her and she started to shout
   When—bingity bang! And the dope gave out.

* Chromatic sounds an octave lower than written.

C. C. Rider  Track 27

This well-known tune is slightly different from the traditional 12-bar blues pattern: the C7 chord is held for an additional measure.

* ⌢ is a *fermata*. Hold this note longer than the note value. (See page 62.)

SCALES

A *scale* is an arrangement of notes that either ascends or descends without skipping or repeating notes. For study purposes, scales begin and end on the same note. For example, a C major scale begins and ends on C, although it may not be the same C.

On this page you'll find the most commonly used major scales. A major scale is "do, re, mi, fa, sol, la, ti, do."

Harmonicas in Different Keys

At this point, you probably only have one or two harmonicas, most likely a C diatonic and/or a C chromatic. As you become better on the instrument, you may want to become more versatile by having several harmonicas in different keys. This way, you can play with other musicians no matter what key they are in.

The most common keys for a blues band would be G, A, E and B♭; the most common keys for a folk band would be C, D, G and A; the most common keys for a rock band would be E, A, G and C; and if the band you're playing with has horns or brass, then the keys F, E♭ and B♭ will be common.

Only some of the following scales can be played on a C diatonic scale; all can be played on a chromatic.

C Major Scale (playable on C diatonic or chromatic harmonica).

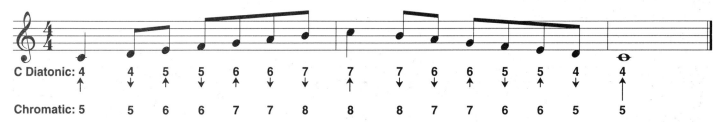

G Major Scale* (playable on G diatonic or chromatic harmonica).

The key signature indicates that every F is to be played as F♯ (F-sharp) unless preceded by a "♮" sign (natural sign).

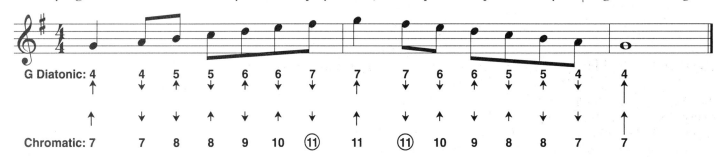

F Major Scale* (playable cross harp on C diatonic, F diatonic or chromatic).

The key signature indicates that every B is to be played B♭ (B-flat) unless preceded by a "♮" sign.

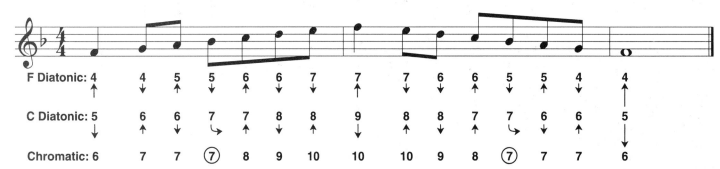

*The notes in these scales sound an octave lower than written.

D Major Scale (playable on D diatonic or chromatic harmonica).

The key signature indicates that
every F is to be played as F♯ and
every C as C♯ unless preceded by a
"♮" sign.

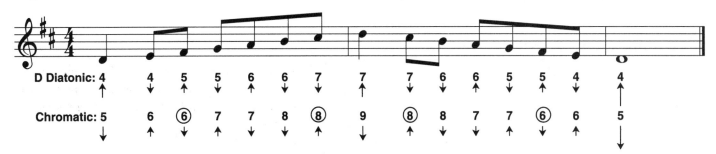

B♭ Major Scale (playable on B♭ diatonic or chromatic harmonica).

The key signature indicates that
every B is to be played as B♭ and
every E as E♭ unless preceded by a
"♮" sign.

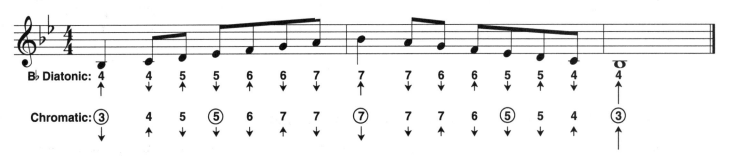

E♭ Major Scale (playable on E♭ diatonic or chromatic harmonica).

The key signature indicates that
every B is to be played as B♭, every E
is played as E♭ and every A is played
as A♭ unless preceded by a "♮" sign.

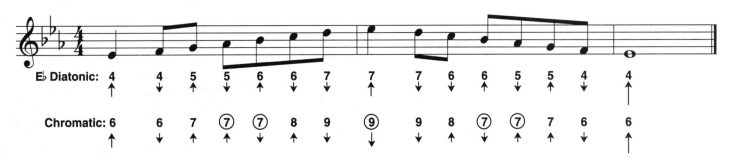

A Major Scale (playable on A diatonic or chromatic harmonica).

The key signature indicates that each
F, C or G is to be played as F♯, C♯ or
G♯ respectively, unless preceded by a
"♮" sign.

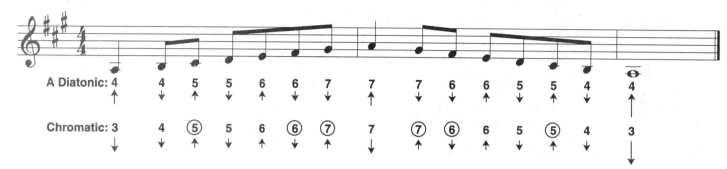

A Diatonic: 4 ↑	4 ↓	5 ↑	5 ↓	6 ↑	6 ↓	7 ↓	7 ↑	7 ↓	6 ↓	6 ↑	5 ↓	5 ↑	4 ↓	4 ↑
Chromatic: 3 ↓	4 ↓	⑤ ↑	5 ↓	6 ↑	⑥ ↓	⑦ ↑	7 ↓	⑦ ↑	⑥ ↓	6 ↑	5 ↓	⑤ ↑	4 ↓	3 ↓

E Major Scale (playable on E diatonic or chromatic harmonica).

The key signature indicates that each
F, C, G or D is to be played as F♯,
C♯, G♯ or D♯ respectively, unless
preceded by a "♮" sign.

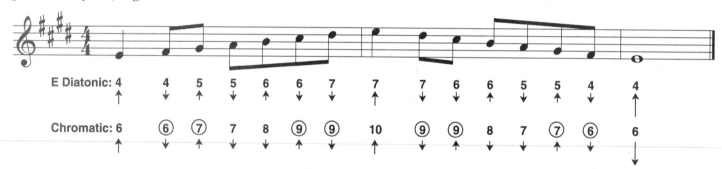

E Diatonic: 4 ↑	4 ↓	5 ↑	5 ↓	6 ↑	6 ↓	7 ↓	7 ↑	7 ↓	6 ↓	6 ↑	5 ↓	5 ↑	4 ↓	4 ↑
Chromatic: 6 ↑	⑥ ↓	⑦ ↑	7 ↓	8 ↓	⑨ ↓	⑨ ↓	10 ↓	⑨ ↓	⑨ ↓	8 ↓	7 ↓	⑦ ↑	⑥ ↓	6 ↓

Bob Dylan

Photograph: Randee St. Nicholas. Photo courtesy of the Institute of Jazz Studies.

BLUES SCALES AND IMPROVISING

When listening to great blues players, perhaps you wonder where these artists 'find' the notes they play? It's obvious that much of what is played on blues and blues-related tunes is improvised—that is, made up on the spur of the moment.

All great players know their scales, and most blues is based on one scale in particular: the pentatonic scale (or blues scale). It's a great scale, because any note you play when improvising is correct. There are no wrong notes! Know this

scale well, and you'll be on your way to playing like the great harp artists.

What About Blues in Other Keys?

Since blues are almost always played on diatonic harmonicas, this chart will show you which harp to use for other keys:

IF THE BLUES IS IN:	USE A HARP IN:
C	F
C♯ or D♭	F♯
D	G
E♭	A♭
E	A
F	B♭
F♯ or G♭	B
G	C
A♭	C♯ or D♭
A	D
B♭	E♭
B	E

PART IV   Styles & Recommended Listening

The harmonica is a flexible and expressive instrument that is suitable for many types of music besides the blues. On the following pages are examples of various styles with hints on how to play them and listening suggestions.

Goin' Down the Road Feelin' Bad   Track 28

This great blues song is based on a 16-bar pattern, a common one in country blues. Play it with a strong rhythmic drive and a little vibrato.

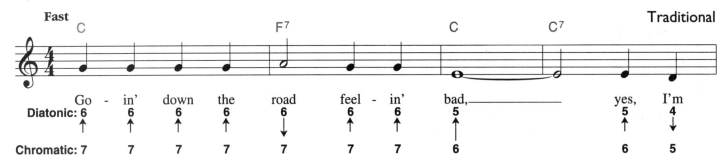

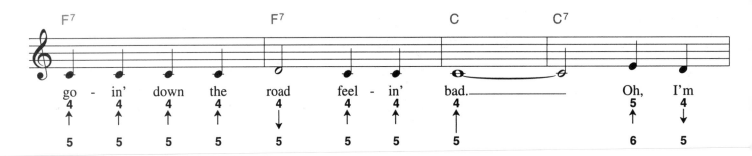

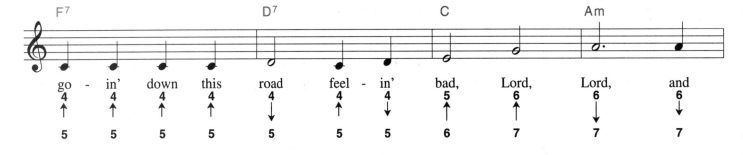

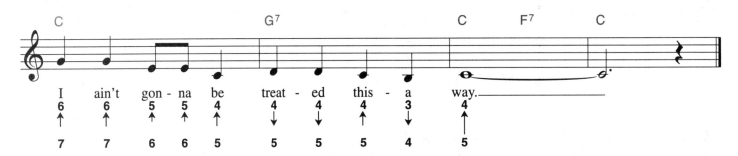

Additional Words
2. Goin' where the climate fits my clothes (3 times)
     And I ain't gonna be treated this-a way.
3. Down in the jail-house on my knees . . .
4. Goin' but I ain't a-comin' back . . .
5. Goin' down the road feelin' bad . . .

La Bamba 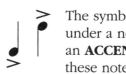 Track 29

This traditional Latin-American dance tune has become a rock standard. Play it with a driving beat. It also includes two new musical signs: the *staccato* and the *accent*. Staccato notes are notes that are played shorter. Try saying "dit" into the harmonica to sound staccato notes. Notes marked with an *accent* > are played louder than others.

Names to listen to in rock: Bruce Springsteen, J. Geils Band and Huey Lewis.

 The symbol > over or under a note indicates an **ACCENT**. Make these notes louder!

A dot over or under a note indicates **STACCATO**. Make these notes very short!

*|: and :| are repeat signs. Play everything between the signs twice. (See page 62.)

Rock-a-My Soul Track 30

Soul music developed from traditional American spirituals like this one. Characteristics of this style include a strong rhythmic drive and accents on the 2nd and 4th beats of the measure. Play this tune cross harp on a C diatonic or on a chromatic.

Names to listen to in soul/R&B: Stevie Wonder and the Blues Brothers.

Aura Lee 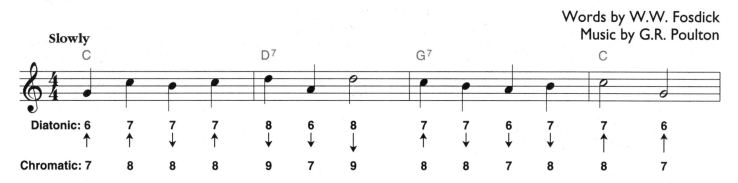 Track 31

This beautiful Civil War ballad was popular with all soldiers. Later it became a graduation song at West Point. But its most popular reincarnation was in 1956 when

Elvis Presley recorded it with a new set of words called *Love Me Tender*. Play it with a good deal of vibrato to bring out the beauty of the melody.

Names to listen to for ballad playing: Woody Guthrie and Pete Seeger.

Words by W.W. Fosdick
Music by G.R. Poulton

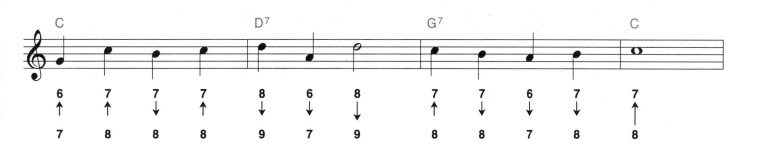

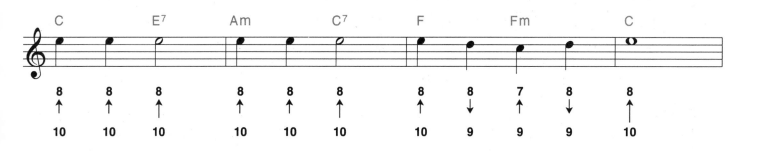

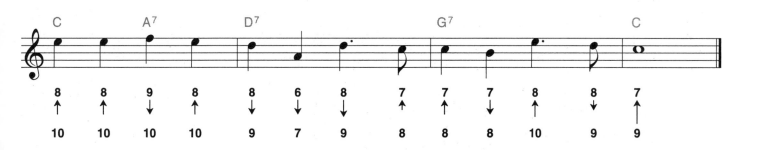

Wildwood Flower Track 32

This country standard was first popularized by the Carter Family back in the '20s and '30s. Heavy vibrato is not appropriate in this type of song. Tempo is brisk and straight ahead. Country names to listen to: Clint Black, Charlie McCoy and Jerry Reed.

Traditional

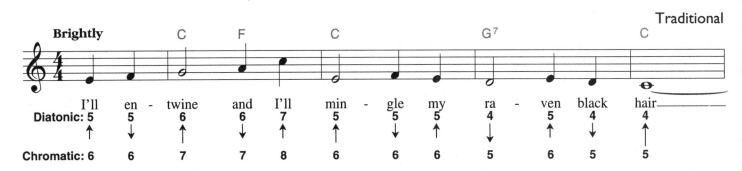

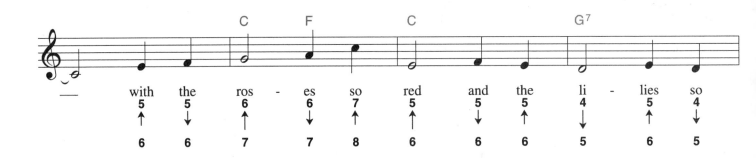

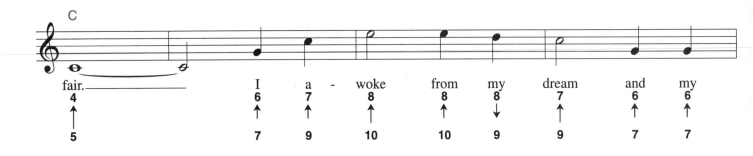

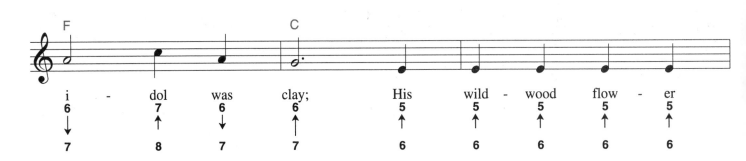

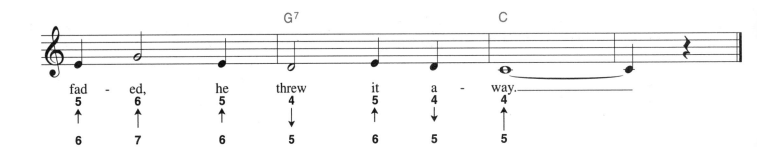

Wabash Cannonball Track 33

Bluegrass has been a popular form of music for over a century and is closely associated with the people of the Appalachian mountains and the south. Shortly before World War II, Earl Flat and Lester Scruggs, Bill Monroe and others made bluegrass more popular to radio listeners all over the country. Their music had a driving, syncopated feel and made it the most exciting form of country music up to that time.

The harmonica and railroads go back a long way together, and this railroad song is one of the great bluegrass standards.

Bluegrass names to listen to: Bill Monroe, Flatt & Scruggs, Bela Fleck and the Flecktones (progressive, somewhat beyond bluegrass).

Traditional

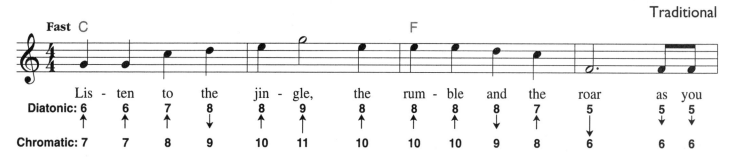

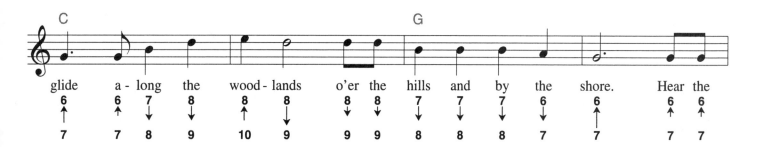

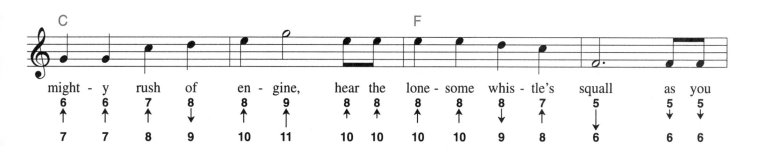

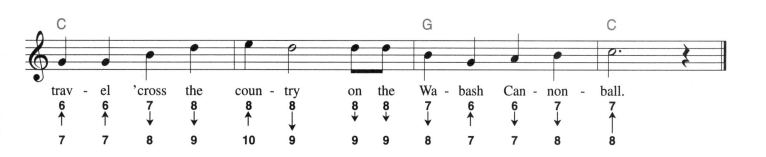

Scarborough Fair Track 34

Although this folk song dates back 400 years, Simon and Garfunkel had one of their biggest hits with it in the 1960s. Play the melody with a pure, even tone and with little vibrato.

Although the key signature would seem to indicate C major, this song is actually based on a type of scale called the *dorian mode*. It consists of the notes D-E-F-G-A-B-C-D, the same notes that are in the C major scale, but with D as the first note instead of C.

Names to listen to in folk: Bob Dylan and Neil Young.

Traditional

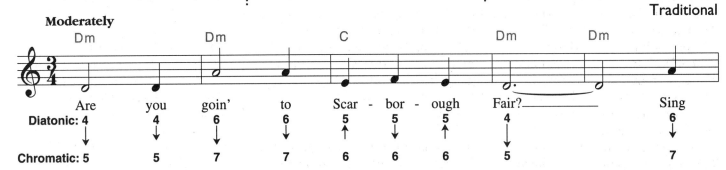

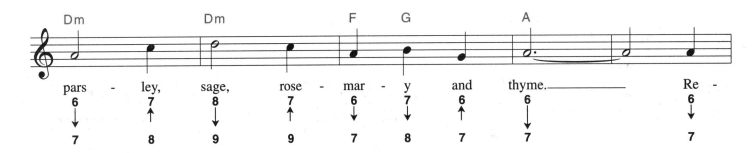

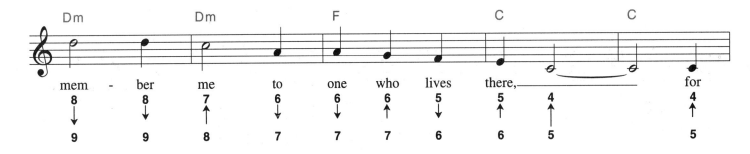

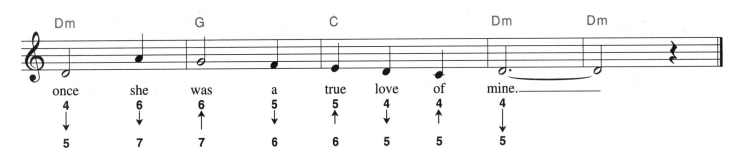

Additional Verses

2. Tell her to buy me an acre of land
   Sing parsley, sage, rosemary and thyme.
   Beneath the wild ocean and yonder sea strand
   And she shall be a true love of mine.

3. Tell her to make me a cambric shirt
   Sing parsley, sage, rosemary and thyme.
   Without any stitching or needlework
   And she shall be a true love of mine.

PART V # More Advanced Techniques

In this section, you'll learn some of the advanced techniques that the pros use. They will be demonstrated through great songs from yesterday and today.

MINI MUSIC LESSON ## GRACE NOTES

Grace notes are notes played very quickly just before the melody note. On harmonica they're usually played by blowing or drawing the hole below the one you actually want, then quickly moving over to the correct hole. On chromatic harp, it's often possible to play the grace note using the slide. The example we've chosen to illustrate this effect is a blues tune, playable on diatonic harp.

Important! The "extra time" needed to play the grace note is taken from the preceding note (not the one following the grace note). You must play the note following the grace note *on time,* without delay (as if the grace note were not there).

In standard notation, the grace note is written as a smaller-sized eighth note with a slash through the stem and flag ♪.

Notice that because this arrangement is played on the lower part of the harmonica, it is written in the bass clef. Here is a review of the bass clef.

Grace-Note Blues   Track 35   by "Tallahassee Red"

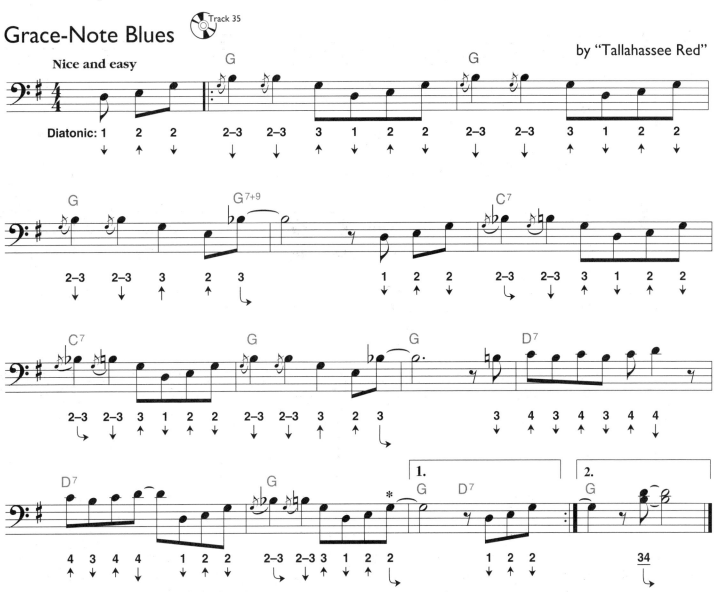

*Bend the note lower and gradually bring it up to pitch.

Sliding

This effect can add spice to your playing. It's simple to do: just blow or draw a hole that's two or three holes away (higher or lower) than the hole you really want to play. Then quickly move to the correct hole. Like the grace note, it's important to land on the final note *on time,* and the time it takes to play the slide is subtracted from the previous note or rest.

In standard notation, the slide is indicated with an angled line and the word "slide" or "sl."

Bill Bailey

Track 36

This famous ragtime song from 1902 uses slides. Because of all the accidentals (sharps or flats that do not appear in the key signature) this arrangement can only be played on the chromatic harp.

Hughie Canon

Battle Hymn of the Republic Track 37

The arrangement of this traditional march includes slides.

Traditional

Choking

The characteristic of the harp that attracts players and listeners right away is its ability to imitate the human voice. One of the ways this is done is by pronouncing various syllables directly into the harp as you play. Here's how to do it:

If you say the word "duck," you'll notice the sound has three parts. First, the tongue is behind the upper teeth. Next, as the "uh" sound is pronounced, the tongue is about halfway in the mouth cavity. Finally, as you say the "ck," the back of the tongue cuts off the air flow from the throat.

Now, keeping the tongue in the back of the throat the way you did for the "ck" sound, play a low draw note, like hole 3. Now draw in hard, and you should get the choked sound heard in blues and rock songs.

The Train Whistle

Using the same tongue position as for "choking," draw hard on holes 4 and 5 (diatonic) or holes 5 and 6 (chromatic). As you draw in the air, say the syllables "too-wee" into the harp. You should get a dip in the pitch at the end of the "too" and then a rise back to the true pitch on the "wee." It will help if you close your lips slightly at the end of the "too" and then open them again on the "wee."

The Yellow Dog Drag  Track 38

The Yellow Dog was hobo slang for the Yazoo Delta Railroad, a short line that used to connect various towns in Mississippi. This blues tune makes use of the effects you just learned.

There is a rhythm you've not yet learned used in this piece called the dotted-8th, 16th-note rhythm

It's played similar to uneven 8th notes or a shuffle. Each group of two notes takes up one beat. A series of dotted 8ths, 16th sounds like "hump-ty dump-ty hump-ty dump-ty." Get this rhythm in your ear before attempting this song:

Hump- ty　dump- ty　hump- ty　dump- ty

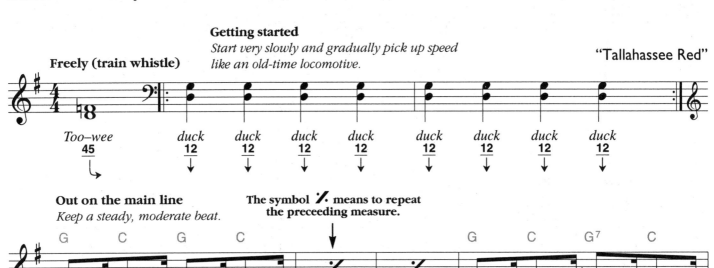

Getting started
Start very slowly and gradually pick up speed like an old-time locomotive.

"Tallahassee Red"

Freely (train whistle)

Too–wee　duck　duck　duck　duck　duck　duck　duck　duck
45　12　12　12　12　12　12　12　12

Out on the main line
Keep a steady, moderate beat.

The symbol 𝄎 means to repeat the preceeding measure.

G　C　G　C　G　C　G⁷　C

34　34 45　45 34　34 45　45　34　34 45　45 45　45 45　45

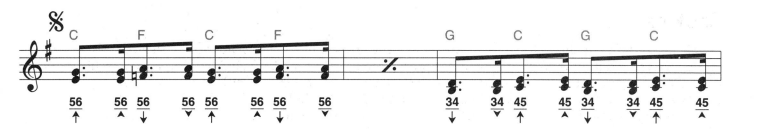

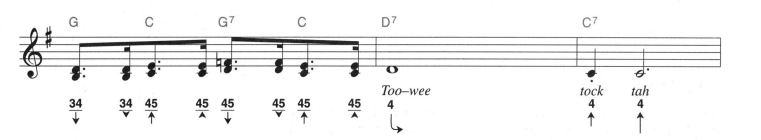

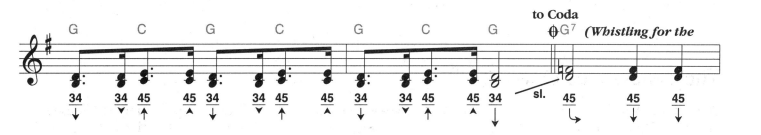

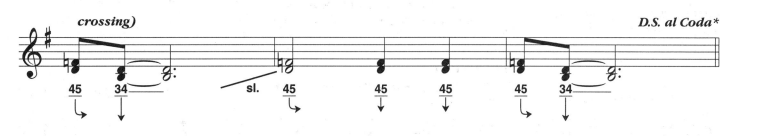

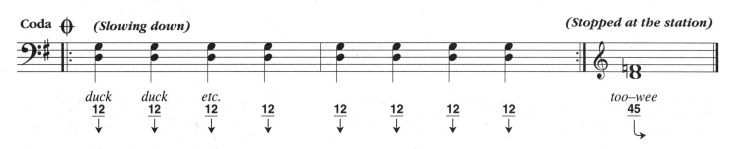

*Read the music as you normally would until you see the "D.S." Then go back to the sign [𝄋] until you reach the second sign [𝄌]. At this sign, you immediately jump to the *Coda* at the end of the tune.

Talking Into the Harp

Saying the syllable "dit" into the harmonica is a useful sound that was introduced with the song *La Bamba* (page 43). To review, say "dit" as a very short sound. If you're doing it right, you'll hear the reeds echoing for a fraction of a second after you cut off the air.

Example 1

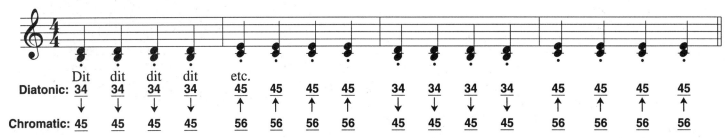

Example 2

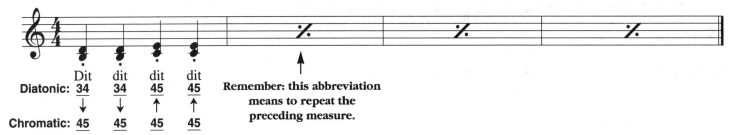

Example 3   Same as Example 2, but twice as fast.

The syllable "toil" is indispensable for playing rock and blues. Practice it similar to the above.

Example 1   Say "toil" on each chord.

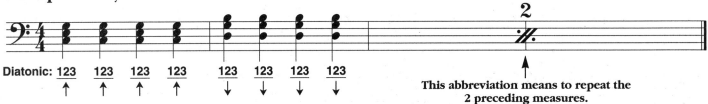

When the tempo starts to get faster, the syllables will sound like "toil-oil-oil-oil."

Example 2

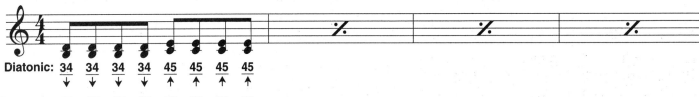

Railroad Bill  Track 39

You can try out the "dit" and "toil" syllables on this famous hobo song. The introduction can be played either as written or using the "dit" syllable.

Stevie Wonder

Photo courtesy of the Institute of Jazz Studies

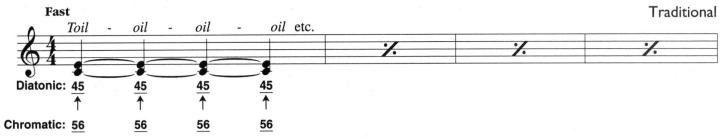

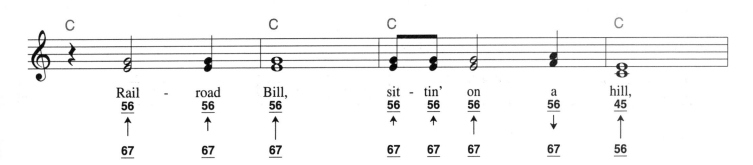

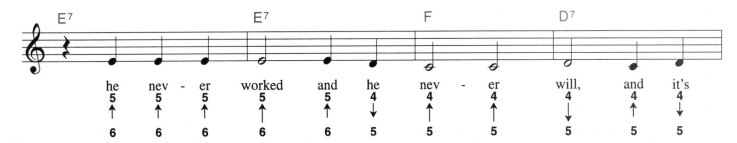

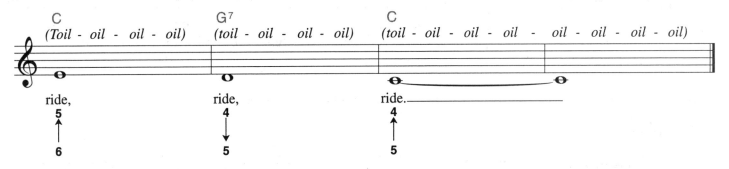

Additional Verse

Railroad Bill, sittin' on a hill,
Lightin' cigars with those ten dollar bills,
And it's ride, ride ride.

Vibrato

On page 5, we brought up the subject of vibrato. There are several ways to produce various types of vibrato, and you should be able to play them all.

Ordinary vibrato is produced when the cupped right hand is opened and then closed around the back of the harmonica. Even this basic technique can be varied to add expressiveness to your tone.

Try this: play a sustained note (blow or draw) and wave the cupped right hand at a fairly rapid speed, about 240 times per minute. You should hear sort of a "wa-wa-wa-wa" sound. At this rapid pace, the right hand should barely move. Now, still holding the tone, gradually slow down the speed of your hand and as you do, increase the distance it moves. You'll hear the "wa-wa-wa-wa" slow down and get wider at the same time. To sum it up, for a fast vibrato, move the right hand only a little; for a slow, wide vibrato, move the hand as much as 2 inches.

How much vibrato you use is a matter of taste. Too little vibrato tends to make music sound cold and unemotional; too much can sound overwrought with insincere feeling. On long held notes, it can be very effective to start the note with almost no vibrato and gradually increase it toward the end of the note.

Now that you're more aware of the uses of vibrato, listen to your favorite players and hear what they do. Imitate what you like and discard what you don't. This is how you'll forge an original style, the goal of every musician.

Other Types of Vibrato

Finger vibrato is a very subtle effect used by some players. To play it, the right hand is shifted around so that the middle finger is lying against the back of the harp. Then, it's an easy matter to wave the finger across the back of the harmonica to create a subtle vibrato, especially on bent blues notes.

Mouth vibrato is accomplished differently. Try this: play a note and hold it. Now pronounce the letter "U" and notice how this produces a waver in the tone. Pronounce a series of U's (like "U-U-U-U"). This type of vibrato, although more difficult to produce, can be very expressive, especially in the lower part of the range.

If you've been producing single notes by the tongue-blocking method, you won't be able to use mouth vibrato, as the tongue is otherwise occupied. Nevertheless, you can still use it when playing chords, as this type of vibrato adds an uncommon beauty to chords played in the lower register.

You can also experiment with other syllables such as "yo," "yoi," "loo," etc. Each one can be used to produce mouth vibrato and has a slightly different effect.

Toots Thielemans

Photo courtesy of the Institute of Jazz Studies.

Danny Boy  Track 40

This traditional Irish melody has several sets of lyrics, but most people know it as *Danny Boy*. The many long-held notes will give you an opportunity to experiment with different types of vibrato.

Melody: Traditional
Words by Fred E. Weatherly

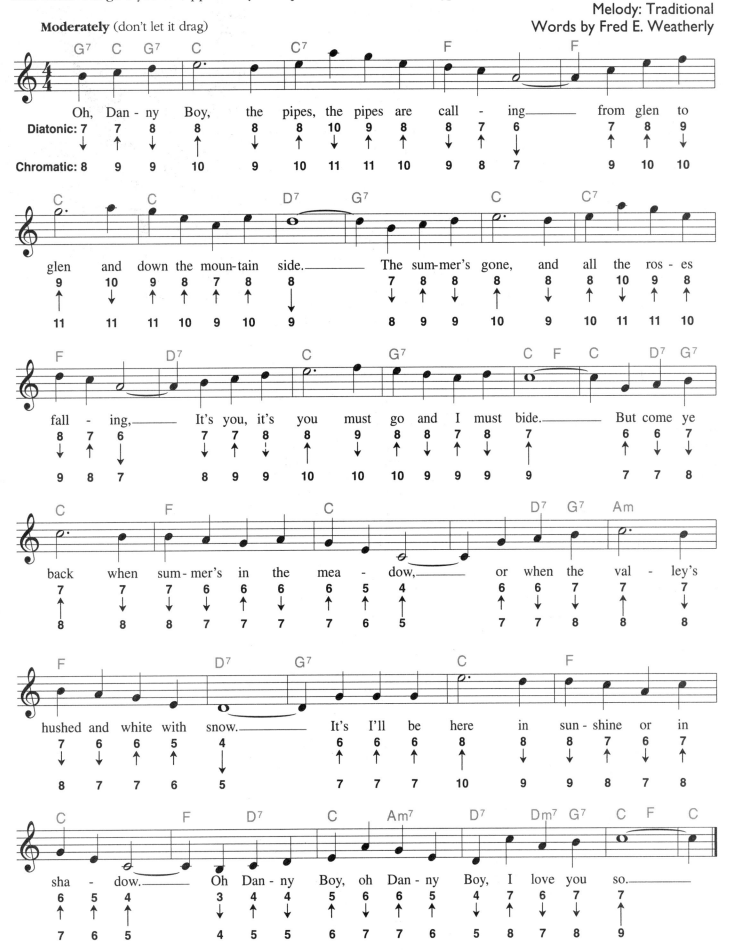

The Shake

The *shake* is another great effect for the harmonica, and is a staple in the repertoire of many great players.

Here's how to do it: blow into hole 5 (hole 6 on chromatic). Without interrupting the flow of air, move the harmonica (not your head) so you're blowing into hole 6 (7 on chromatic). Now go back to hole 5 (6). Keep alternating between the two holes without interrupting the air flow. Now try the same effect on draw notes, say 3 and 4 on diatonic or 4 and 5 on chromatic. That's all there is to it!

In standard music notation, the shake is written as this:

As easy as this effect is to produce, it's invaluable for creating backgrounds in group playing. For example, here's a typical background for the blues in G played cross harp on either a C diatonic or chromatic.

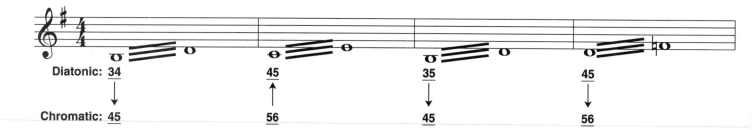

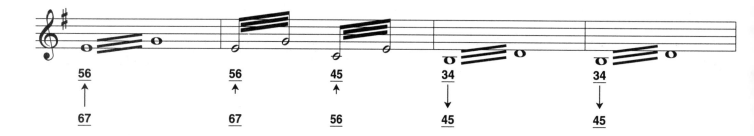

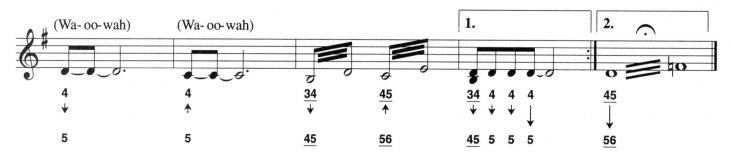

Although the above has no melody of its own, it is a perfect example of what to play when somebody else is playing a solo.

 SYNCOPATION

Syncopation is the name given to a musical effect in which a note is anticipated, that is, played before the beat. For example, this rhythm is not syncopated—each quarter note falls in the expected place, *on* the beat.

The following example uses syncopation. The 3rd quarter note is played on the "and" of the 2nd beat, rather than its expected place on the 3rd beat. For best results, count carefully and accent (> = play a little louder) all syncopated notes.

Since the days of ragtime in the late 19th century, syncopation has been an important component in every kind of American music—including Dixieland, swing, rock, blues, country and folk—and is also very important in all of the Latin and Caribbean styles such as rhumba, cha-cha, bossa nova, reggae, ska and salsa. Although a thorough study of syncopation is beyond the scope of this book, the exercises below will introduce you to this essential subject. Serious musicians cannot expect to succeed in popular music without a thorough understanding of syncopation.

Play the following exercises on E (blow hole 8 on diatonic or hole 10 on chromatic). After you get comfortable with the rhythms, try making up your own tunes using these syncopations.

The Entertainer Track 41

Scott Joplin was one of America's most original and prolific composers, considered by many to be one of the founders of ragtime. In the 1970s, this rag was used in the movie *The Sting*, which led to a rediscovery of Joplin's music and a new appreciation for his genius.

Because of the many sharps and flats, it's only possible to play this song on a chromatic harmonica.

Scott Joplin

Illustration: Ted Engelbart

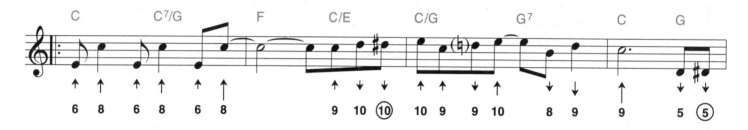

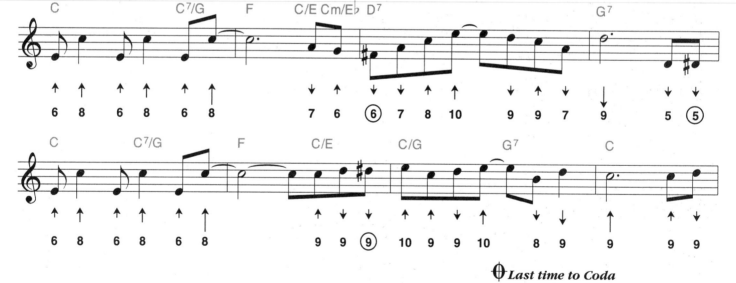

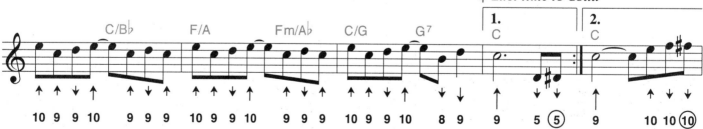

*If you don't have holes 13 and 14 on your chromatic harmonica, play this first measure the same as the second.

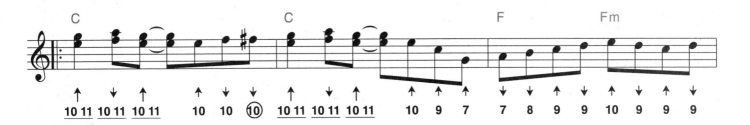

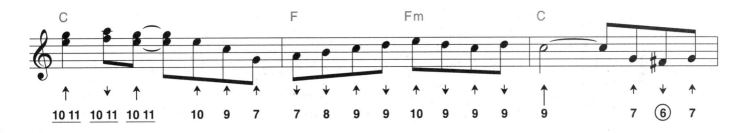

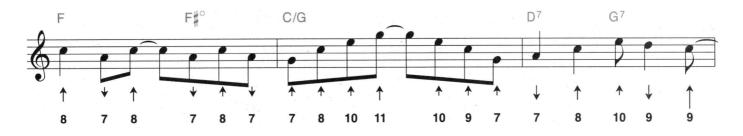

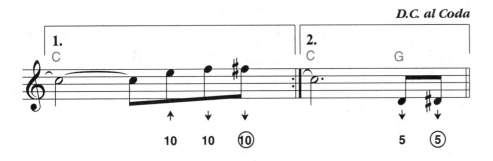

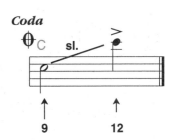

BASIC MUSICAL SYMBOLS RECAP

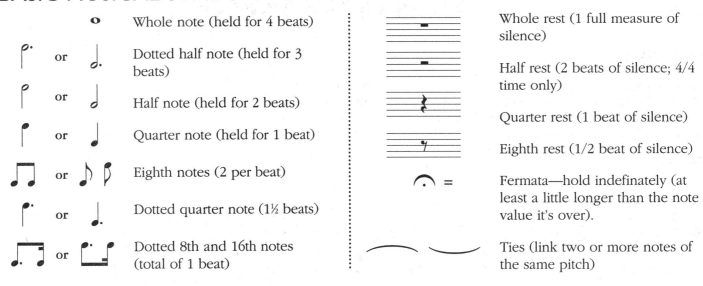

o	Whole note (held for 4 beats)
𝅗𝅥. or 𝅗𝅥.	Dotted half note (held for 3 beats)
𝅗𝅥 or 𝅗𝅥	Half note (held for 2 beats)
𝅘𝅥 or 𝅘𝅥	Quarter note (held for 1 beat)
𝅘𝅥𝅮𝅘𝅥𝅮 or 𝅘𝅥𝅮 𝅘𝅥𝅮	Eighth notes (2 per beat)
𝅘𝅥. or 𝅘𝅥.	Dotted quarter note (1½ beats)
𝅘𝅥𝅮. 𝅘𝅥𝅯 or 𝅘𝅥𝅮. 𝅘𝅥𝅯	Dotted 8th and 16th notes (total of 1 beat)

▬	Whole rest (1 full measure of silence)
▬	Half rest (2 beats of silence; 4/4 time only)
𝄾	Quarter rest (1 beat of silence)
𝄿	Eighth rest (1/2 beat of silence)
𝄐 =	Fermata—hold indefinately (at least a little longer than the note value it's over).
⌣ ⌣	Ties (link two or more notes of the same pitch)

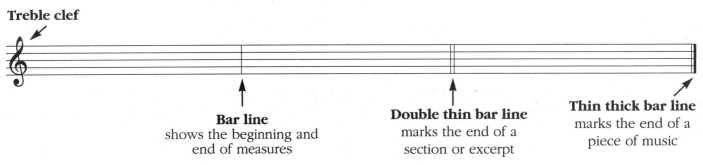

Treble clef

Bar line
shows the beginning and end of measures

Double thin bar line
marks the end of a section or excerpt

Thin thick bar line
marks the end of a piece of music

/ means "repeat preceding chord"

✕. means "repeat preceding measure"

✕✕. means "repeat two preceding measures"

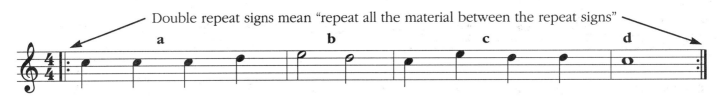

Double repeat signs mean "repeat all the material between the repeat signs"

a   b   c   d

In the example above you would play measures a b c d a b c d.

1st and 2nd endings are used to indicate partial repeats.

a   b   c   1. d   2. e

In the example above you would play measures a b c d a b c e.

Key signatures

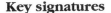

C major or A minor	D major or B minor	F major or D minor	G major or E minor	A major or F♯ minor	B♭ major or G minor	E♭ major or C minor

PART VI Licks in the Style Of . . .

THE BEATLES

The Beatles, one of the most influential rock groups ever, started with the blues and took pop music to another level. Here are a few licks to be played on a diatonic, except No. 3, a pretty ballad that needs to be played on a chromatic.

*Quarter note triplet=three notes in two beats.

Licks in the Style of
BOB DYLAN

Bob Dylan came to prominence in the early '60s as a folk performer. Dylan's simple harmonica licks add to his incisive lyrics and supportive guitar playing. The licks below are in the style of some of Dylan's best-known early hits.

These licks are based on a variation of the 12-bar blues progression. Notice measures 9 and 10 especially.

Licks in the Style of
BRUCE SPRINGSTEEN

Bruce Springsteen's powerful lyrics and hard-driving tunes are among the most listened to and admired in rock music, and he often spices up his songs with harmonica. Here are a couple of samples in his style that run from sweet and soulful to funky and blues-drenched.

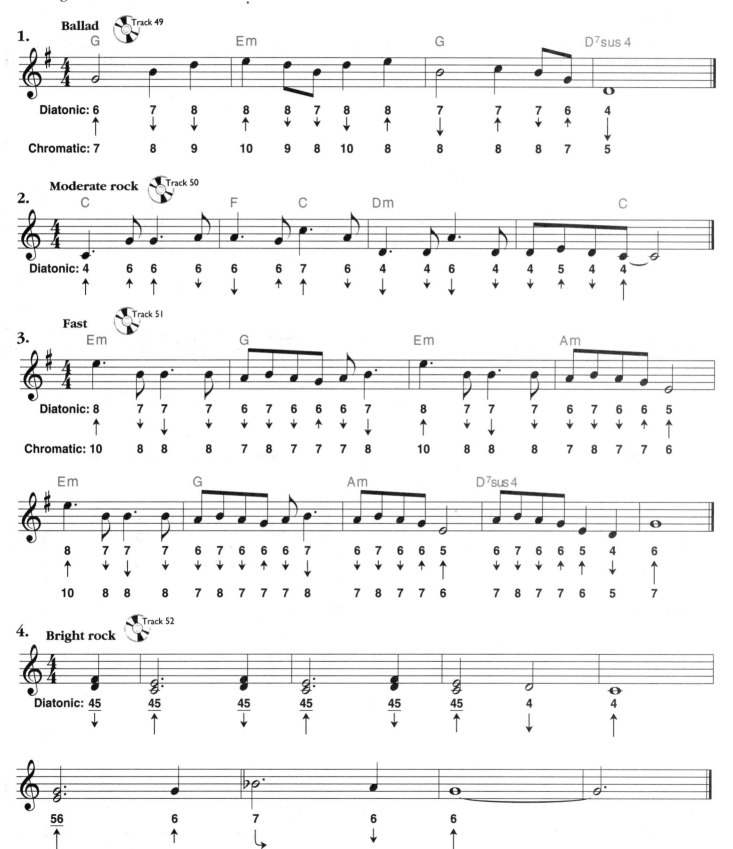

Licks in the Style of
BILLY JOEL

In 1973, Billy Joel landed into pop stardom with his first big hit, *Piano Man* from the album of the same name. A soulful harmonica part on this tune and others such as the memorable *Billy the Kid* helped launch a career that is still going strong today.

Licks in the Style of
STEVIE WONDER

Known in the early days as "Little Stevie Wonder," it was clear that this man was going to be a major force in music. Combing his formidable skills on keyboard and harmonica, his career as an innovator continues to this day.

These licks are all based on the G blues scale (see p. 41). As you know, these licks will fit with any blues or blues-influenced tune in the key of G. Since Stevie's style is complicated rhythmically, the arrows only indicate whether to

blow, draw or bend the note, and do not exactly reflect the note's rhythmic value.

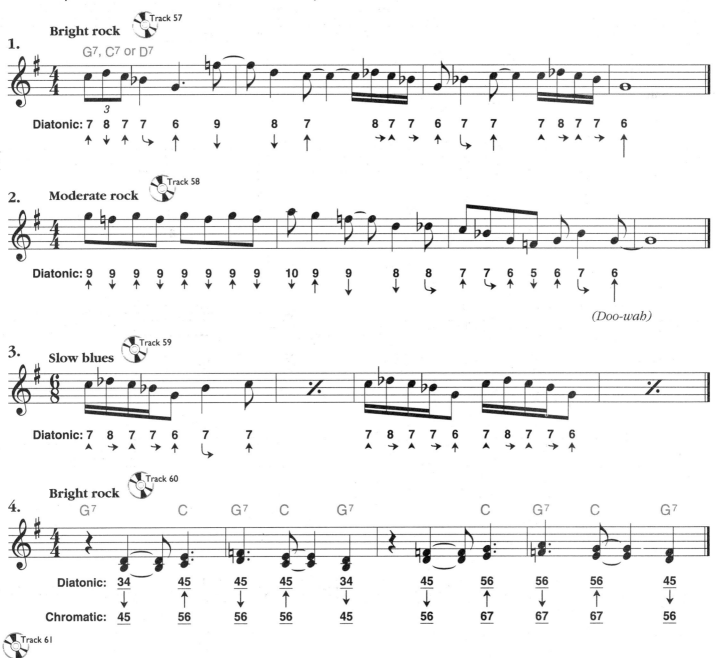

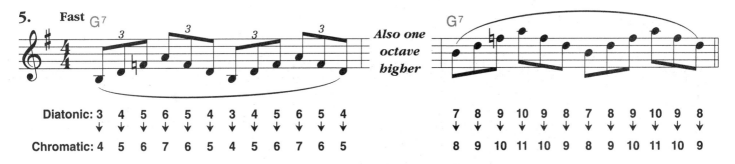

These licks are played like a slide. Start to draw hole 3 (4 on the chromatic) and move the harp back and forth.

Licks in the Style of

HUEY LEWIS

Huey Lewis and the News broke into the scene in 1980 with a hot hit called *Workin' for a Livin'* featuring Huey's harmonica playing. He and the band have enjoyed a string of hits since, some of which continue to feature his Paul Butterfield-inspired blues harmonica playing.

Sometimes called "3rd position," this cross-harp arrangement is actually in the key of D, but is played on a C harp.

Licks in the Style of

THE J. GEILS BAND

Since the 1970s, the J. Geils Band has been a powerhouse of great upbeat R&B-influenced music. Their band features a full-time harmonica player, Magic Dick, who is one of the living greats of the instrument. The licks in his style are blues-based and are played cross harp.

In this example, each measure is played on one long breath as the harp is moved back and forth from hole to hole. This effect is similar to the shake discussed on page 58.

This lick makes ingenious use of the same note (low G), which can be played two different ways. Follow the numbers carefully.

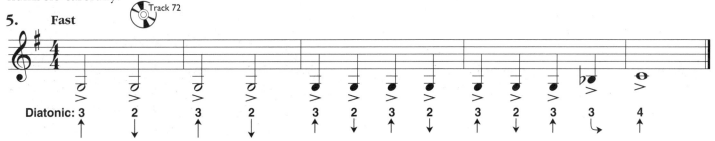

PART VII

Final Thoughts

Playing with a Band

Playing with a band is probably the most fun you can have with a harmonica, but there are a few things you should keep in mind:

1. Make sure the instruments are in tune. Most bands tune to the note A, which is draw 6 on diatonic and draw 7 on chromatic. Since the harmonica is tuned at the factory, it can't be altered. Other instruments (bass and guitar, for example) must tune to you. Some electric keyboards can be tuned on the spot, but acoustic pianos cannot. If your harmonica doesn't sound in tune with the piano, there's nothing to be done, and it's better not to play at all. (Better that than sound horrible—the audience won't know what's going on; they'll only know you sound bad!)

2. Make sure you have a harmonica in the key the band is playing in. If you're playing chromatic, you won't have any problem. But it's embarrassing to have the band play a tune in E♭, say, and there you are without an E♭ diatonic harp. Or, if you're playing cross harp and have a C, D and G blues harp with you, make sure the band plays in G, A or D. Get this straightened out before playing. Incidentally, it's pretty dark in most clubs, so it's a good idea to put large labels on each harp so you can identify keys.

3. Although your harp may sound loud to you at home, in a club it's probably not loud enough to be heard over the band. However, the harp is easy to play through a microphone. A chromatic harp is usually played through a vocal mike on its own stand, so you can work the slide without worrying about dropping the mike or the harp. You can play a diatonic the same way, or you can hold the mike and harp in your cupped hands. If you're serious about your playing, you can invest in your own mike and amplifier. (Talk to your local music dealer for recommendations on the appropriate gear.)

One final thought: the most important thing in playing with a group is not to let your ego get in the way. Playing blues and rock is a group process and requires communication and cooperation among musicians. Listen to what the guitarist is doing and leave him room for leads. Try to make a unified, whole sound. Nothing ruins a musical experience and a group as much as when everyone tries to be the star. If you can keep that in mind, and if you can wail pretty well, you'll be a much-in-demand harpist.

J. Geils Band

Photo: David Gahr.
Photo courtesy of the Institute of Jazz Studies.

Answers to Riddles and Quizzes

1. A BEADED BAG   2. A FADED BADGE   3. A CAB   4. DEAF   5. BAD EGG   6. GABE GABBED

1.

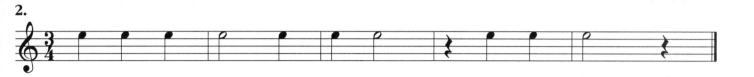

2.

3.

Blues Progressions in Various Keys

Blues in D (use a G diatonic)

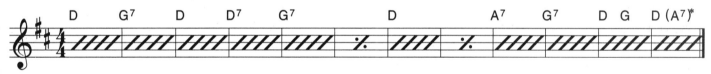

$\diagup$ = *slash notation.* This means play the chord written above the staff once for each $\diagup$.

Blues in C (use a F diatonic)

Blues in A (use a D diatonic)

Blues in F (use a B♭ diatonic)

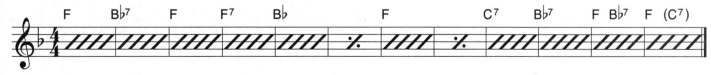

*Chords in parentheses are played only when repeating back to the beginning.

Master Chart of Notes on the Harmonica